D0149342

A FUTURE AS
BRIGHT
AS YOUR FAITH

COUNSEL AND INSPIRATION
FOR EACH DAY OF THE YEAR

THOMAS S. MONSON

DESERET
BOOK

SALT LAKE CITY, UTAH

Library of Congress Cataloging-in-Publication Data

Monson, Thomas S., 1927– author.
  A future as bright as your faith / Thomas S. Monson.
     pages cm
  Counsel and inspiration for each day of the year.
  Includes bibliographical references.
  ISBN 978-1-62972-113-2 (hardbound : alk. paper)
  1. Devotional calendars—The Church of Jesus Christ of Latter-day Saints. 2. Christian life—Mormon authors. 3. Mormons—Conduct of life. 4. Devotional calendars. I. Title.
  BX8656.M657 2015
  242'.2—dc23   2015015044

Printed in Canada
Friesens, Manitoba, Canada

10 9 8 7 6 5 4 3 2 1

JANUARY

*Wherefore, ye must press forward with a
steadfastness in Christ, having a perfect
brightness of hope, and a love of God and
of all men. Wherefore, if ye shall press
forward, feasting upon the word of Christ,
and endure to the end, behold, thus saith
the Father: Ye shall have eternal life.*

2 Nephi 31:20

A FUTURE AS BRIGHT AS YOUR FAITH

And Jesus answering saith unto them,
Have faith in God.

MARK 11:22

I testify to you that our promised blessings are beyond measure. Though the storm clouds may gather, though the rains may pour down upon us, our knowledge of the gospel and our love of our Heavenly Father and of our Savior will comfort and sustain us and bring joy to our hearts as we walk uprightly and keep the commandments. There will be nothing in this world that can defeat us.

My beloved brothers and sisters, fear not. Be of good cheer. The future is as bright as your faith.

FOUR PLEDGES FOR THE NEW YEAR

*Verily, verily, I say unto you, even as you desire of me
so it shall be done unto you; and, if you desire, you shall
be the means of doing much good in this generation.*

DOCTRINE AND COVENANTS 11:8

Four pledges for the new year: *I will listen,
I will learn, I will labor, I will love.* As we fulfill
these pledges, we can have the guidance of our
Heavenly Father and in our own lives experience true joy. Now, I don't simply mean that we
should make a wish, or that we should dream a
dream, but rather determine to do that which
we pledge to accomplish.

A DESTINY TO FULFILL

But ye are a chosen generation, a royal priesthood,
an holy nation, a peculiar people; that ye should
shew forth the praises of him who hath called you
out of darkness into his marvellous light.

1 PETER 2:9

You are the sons and daughters of Almighty God. You have a destiny to fulfill, a life to live, a contribution to make, a goal to achieve. The future of the kingdom of God upon the earth will, in part, be aided by your devotion.

When this perspective is firmly in mind, you can appreciate the absolute necessity of diligence in this, your period of preparation. Neglect to prepare and you mortgage your future.

THE OPEN ROAD OF LIFE

And they did press forward through the mist of darkness, clinging to the rod of iron, even until they did come forth and partake of the fruit of the tree.

1 NEPHI 8:24

Ahead is the open road. Those who walk it successfully ignore irrelevant attractions and refrain from activities which do not contribute to attainment of their purpose. They disregard the billboards designed to divert them into this or that blind alley of ease and pleasure. They stand on their own feet, set their own goals, and win their own victories.

ESCAPE TEMPTATION

Blessed is the man that endureth temptation:
for when he is tried, he shall receive the crown of life,
which the Lord hath promised to them that love him.

JAMES 1:12

There hath no temptation taken you but such as is common to man: but God is faithful, who will not suffer you to be tempted above that ye are able; but will with the temptation also make a way to escape, that ye may be able to bear it" (1 Corinthians 10:13).

We do not quote that scripture very frequently these days. Rather, we prefer to echo the words used on television by a comedian: "The devil made me do it!" I think a lot of people like to say, "The devil made me do it," rather than admitting that for every temptation that comes to man, there is a way to escape the temptation.

LOVE FOR OUR FELLOWMEN

*And he answering said, Thou shalt love
the Lord thy God with all thy heart, and with
all thy soul, and with all thy strength, and with
all thy mind; and thy neighbour as thyself.*

LUKE 10:27

Man, by nature, is tempted to seek only his own glory and not the glory of his neighbor or the glory of his God. None of us lives alone—in our city, our nation, or our world. There is no dividing line between our prosperity and our neighbor's wretchedness.

THE GREATEST SINGLE LESSON

For that which ye have seen me do even
that shall ye do; Therefore, if ye do these things blessed
are ye, for ye shall be lifted up at the last day.

3 Nephi 27:21–22

Remember that ofttimes the wisdom of God appears as foolishness to men, but the greatest single lesson we can learn in mortality is that when God speaks and a man obeys, that man will always be right.

May we ever follow the Prince of Peace, who literally showed the way for us to follow, for by doing so, we will survive these turbulent times. His divine plan can save us from the dangers which surround us on every side. His example points the way. When faced with temptation, He shunned it. When offered the world, He declined it. When asked for His life, He gave it.

A LEGACY OF LOVE

Beloved, if God so loved us,
we ought also to love one another.

1 JOHN 4:11

Seemingly little lessons of love are observed by children as they silently absorb the examples of their parents. Let us make certain that our examples are worthy of emulation. When our homes carry the legacy of love, we will not receive Jacob's chastisement as recorded in the Book of Mormon: "Ye have broken the hearts of your tender wives, and lost the confidence of your children, because of your bad examples before them; and the sobbings of their hearts ascend up to God against you" (Jacob 2:35).

Rather, may our families and homes be filled with love: love of each other, love of the gospel, love of our fellowman, and love of our Savior.

OUR RESPONSIBILITY TO CHOOSE

Therefore, cheer up your hearts, and remember that ye are free to act for yourselves—to choose the way of everlasting death or the way of eternal life.

2 NEPHI 10:23

We have the right to choose; likewise, we have the responsibility to choose. We cannot be neutral. There is no middle ground. The Lord knows this; Lucifer knows this. So the Lord has prepared His road signs for our guidance. They read: "Fear God, and keep his commandments" (Ecclesiastes 12:13). Another: "Whatsoever ye sow, that shall ye also reap" (D&C 6:33).

COURAGE

Be strong and of a good courage.

JOSHUA 1:6

Courage is the word we need to hear and hold near our hearts—courage to turn our backs on temptation, courage to lift up our voices in testimony to all whom we meet, remembering that everyone must have an opportunity to hear the message. It is not an easy thing for most to do this. But we can come to believe in the words of Paul to Timothy: "For God hath not given us the spirit of fear; but of power, and of love, and of a sound mind. Be not thou therefore ashamed of the testimony of our Lord" (2 Timothy 1:7–8).

MOMENTS
OF MEDITATION

*Lay not up for yourselves treasures upon earth, where moth
and rust doth corrupt, and where thieves break through and
steal: But lay up for yourselves treasures in heaven, . . .
For where your treasure is, there will your heart be also.*

MATTHEW 6:19–21

Everywhere people are in a hurry. Jet-powered aircraft speed their precious human cargo across broad continents and vast oceans so that business meetings might be attended, obligations met, vacations enjoyed, or families visited. Roadways everywhere—including freeways, thruways, and motorways—carry millions of automobiles, occupied by more millions of people, in a seemingly endless stream and for a multitude of reasons as we rush about the business of each day.

In this fast-paced life, do we ever pause for moments of meditation—even thoughts of timeless truths?

DOING OUR BEST

Do not run faster or labor more
than you have strength . . . ;
but be diligent unto the end.

DOCTRINE AND COVENANTS 10:4

May we be persistent in those things which are good and noble. May we ever stay safely on the Lord's side of the line. May we be considerate, studious, responsive to the whisperings of the Holy Spirit. May we be dedicated to the gospel of Jesus Christ. May we love one another and always look for the best in people. May we do our best in all that we do.

A PERIOD OF PREPARATION

*Know ye not that they which run
in a race run all, but one receiveth the prize?
So run, that ye may obtain.*

1 CORINTHIANS 9:24

The race of life is so important, the prize so valued, that great emphasis must necessarily be placed on adequate and thorough preparation.

When we contemplate the eternal nature of our choices, preparation is a vital factor in our lives. The day will come when we will look upon our period of preparation and be grateful that we properly applied ourselves.

LIVES THAT REFLECT GOSPEL TEACHINGS

And ye became followers of us,
and of the Lord, having received the word in much
affliction, with joy of the Holy Ghost: So that
ye were ensamples to all that believe.

1 THESSALONIANS 1:6–7

Most of those who embrace the message of the missionaries have had other exposures to The Church of Jesus Christ of Latter-day Saints—perhaps hearing the magnificent Tabernacle Choir perform, or just knowing another person who is a member and for whom respect exists. We, as members, should be at our best. Our lives should reflect the teachings of the gospel, and our hearts and voices ever be ready to share the truth.

EVERY MEMBER NEEDED

*And they who were baptized
in the name of Jesus were called
the church of Christ.*

3 NEPHI 26:21

The Church has need of every member! Church leaders and members alike need to give acceptance and full fellowship to singles— all of them: the never married, the widowed, and the divorced. They need to be lifted up in their own self-image and in the eyes of others. The Church setting for them needs to be one of caring, nurturing, and involvement. Let us remember that everyone is a member of a family, even though everyone does not happen to be married.

SAVIORS ON MOUNT ZION

*But of him are ye in Christ Jesus, who of God
is made unto us wisdom, and righteousness,
and sanctification, and redemption.*

1 CORINTHIANS 1:30

Great service is given when we perform vicarious ordinances for those who have gone beyond the veil. In many cases we do not know those for whom we perform the work. We expect no thanks, nor do we have the assurance that they will accept that which we offer. However, we serve, and in that process we attain that which comes of no other effort: we literally become saviors on Mount Zion. As our Savior gave His life as a vicarious sacrifice for us, so we, in some small measure, do the same when we perform proxy work in the temple.

A FORMULA FOR LIFE

But ye will teach them to walk in the ways of truth and soberness; ye will teach them to love one another, and to serve one another.

MOSIAH 4:15

May I leave with you a simple yet far-reaching formula to guide you in the choices of life:

Fill your minds with truth.

Fill your hearts with love.

Fill your lives with service.

By doing so, may we one day hear the plaudit from our Lord and Savior, "Well done, good and faithful servant; thou hast been faithful over a few things, I will make thee ruler over many things: enter thou into the joy of thy lord" (Matthew 25:23).

GENUINE RESPECT BUILDS HAPPINESS

Let each esteem other better than themselves.

PHILIPPIANS 2:3

Happiness abounds when there is genuine respect one for another. Wives draw closer to their husbands, and husbands are more appreciative of their wives, and children are happy, as children are meant to be. Where there is respect in the home, children do not find themselves in that dreaded "never never land"—never the object of concern, never the recipient of proper parental guidance.

A Watchword to Success

*Finally, be ye all of one mind, having compassion
one of another, love as brethren, be pitiful, be courteous.*

1 Peter 3:8

Basic courtesy is required of you and me. There isn't room for anger, there isn't room for disappointment. I think it is far better to be courteous to all around us and make that second effort than to fly off the handle and show our displeasure through a lack of tact and a lack of good self-discipline. Let us be courteous to all of our associates, to subordinates, to superiors, and we shall indeed find it is one of the watchwords to success.

EXPRESSING GRATITUDE

*And it came to pass that he built an altar
of stones, and made an offering unto the Lord,
and gave thanks unto the Lord our God.*

1 Nephi 2:7

The United States Post Office dead-letter department receives annually thousands and thousands of children's pre-Christmas letters addressed to Santa Claus asking for things. After it was all over one year, a single, solitary letter thanking Santa Claus was received. Could this be one of the problems of this troubled world; that people think only of getting—not giving? Of receiving—and not even expressing their gratitude for that which they do receive?

LABOR WITH LOVE

And we have known and believed the love that
God hath to us. God is love; and he that dwelleth
in love dwelleth in God, and God in him.

1 JOHN 4:16

There is no substitute for love. Often this love is kindled in youth by a mother, expanded by a father, and kept vibrant through service to God. Remember the Lord's counsel: "And faith, hope, charity and love, with an eye single to the glory of God, qualify him for the work" (D&C 4:5). Well might each of us ask himself: *Today, have I increased in faith, in hope, in charity, in love?* When our lives comply with God's standard and we labor with love to bring souls unto Him, those within our sphere of influence will never speak the lament, "The harvest is past, the summer is ended, and we are not saved" (Jeremiah 8:20).

STRETCHING OUR MENTAL MUSCLES

Study and learn, and become acquainted with all good books, and with languages, tongues, and people.

DOCTRINE AND COVENANTS 90:15

Reading "out of the best books" stretches our mental muscles and expands our horizons. It takes us out of our mundane worlds and lets us travel as far as our imaginations and the picture painting words of the authors can carry us. Reading keeps us vibrant, it keeps us alive and makes us far more interesting to our marriage mates and our families. It is also a form of insurance against mental aging. We are only as old as we think we are. Some people say that one way to keep alive is to keep interested in many things, and the way to keep interested is to read widely and wisely.

THE MEANING OF LIVING

And let us not be weary in well doing:
for in due season we shall reap, if we faint not.

GALATIANS 6:9

To measure the goodness of life by its delights and pleasures is to apply a false standard. The abundant life does not consist of a glut of luxury. It does not make itself content with commercially produced pleasure, mistaking it for joy and happiness.

To find real happiness, we must seek for it in a focus outside ourselves. No one has learned the meaning of living until he has surrendered his ego to the service of his fellowmen. Service to others is akin to duty, the fulfillment of which brings true joy.

LEARN TO PRAY BY PRAYING

And the twelve did teach the multitude; and behold, they did cause that the multitude should kneel down upon the face of the earth, and should pray unto the Father in the name of Jesus.

3 NEPHI 19:6

We learn to pray by praying. One can devote countless hours to examining the experiences of others, but nothing penetrates the human heart as does a personal, fervent prayer and its heaven-sent response.

Such was the example of the boy Samuel. Such was the experience of young Nephi. Such was the far-reaching prayer of the youth Joseph Smith. Such can be the blessing of one who prays.

MAGNIFY YOUR CALLING

*For though I preach the gospel, I have
nothing to glory of: for necessity is laid upon me;
yea, woe is unto me, if I preach not the gospel!*

1 CORINTHIANS 9:16

Avoid the temptation of ladder climbing in the mission leadership ranks. It matters little whether you are a district or zone leader or assistant to the president. The important thing is that each one does his very best in the work to which he has been called. Why, I had some missionaries who were so adept at training new missionaries that I couldn't spare them for other leadership assignments.

WHAT THE WORLD NEEDS

Wherefore, go to, and call servants, that we may labor diligently with our might in the vineyard, that we may prepare the way, that I may bring forth again the natural fruit, which natural fruit is good and the most precious above all other fruit.

JACOB 5:61

A dictionary defines a pioneer as "one who goes before to prepare or open up the way for others to follow" (*Oxford English Dictionary*, "pioneer"). Can we somehow muster the courage and steadfastness of purpose that characterized the pioneers of a former generation? Can you and I, in actual fact, be pioneers?

I know we can be. Oh, how the world needs pioneers today!

A DETERMINATION TO SERVE

Be not weary in well-doing, for ye are laying
the foundation of a great work. And out of small
things proceedeth that which is great. Behold,
the Lord requireth the heart and a willing mind.

DOCTRINE AND COVENANTS 64:33–34

Though exaltation is a personal matter, and while individuals are saved not as a group but indeed as individuals, yet one cannot live in a vacuum. Membership in the Church calls forth a determination to serve. A position of responsibility may not be of recognized importance, nor may the reward be broadly known. Service, to be acceptable to the Savior, must come from willing minds, ready hands, and pledged hearts.

HELP FOR
THOSE IN NEED

*And God is able to make all grace abound
toward you; that ye, always having all sufficiency
in all things, may abound to every good work.*

2 CORINTHIANS 9:8

There are those throughout the world who are hungry; there are those who are destitute. Working together, we can alleviate suffering and provide for those in need. In addition to the service you give as you care for another, your contributions to the funds of the Church enable us to respond almost immediately when disasters occur anywhere in the world. We are nearly always among the first on the scene to provide whatever assistance we can. We thank you for your generosity.

TWO QUESTIONS EACH OF US MUST ANSWER

Draw near unto me and I will draw near unto you;
seek me diligently and ye shall find me; ask, and ye
shall receive; knock, and it shall be opened unto you.

DOCTRINE AND COVENANTS 88:63

Pitied is the hand that sins. Envied is the hand that paints. Honored is the hand that builds. Appreciated is the hand that helps. Respected is the hand that serves. Adored is the hand that saves—even the hand of Jesus Christ, the Son of God, the Redeemer of all mankind. With that hand He knocks upon the door of our understanding.

"Behold, I stand at the door, and knock: if any man hear my voice, and open the door, I will come in to him" (Revelation 3:20).

Shall we listen for His voice? Shall we open the doorway of our lives to His exalted presence?

THE RACE OF LIFE

*Be of good courage, and he shall strengthen
your heart, all ye that hope in the Lord.*

PSALM 31:24

Each of us is a runner in the race of life. Comforting is the fact that there are many runners. Reassuring is the knowledge that our eternal Scorekeeper is understanding. Challenging is the truth that each must run. But you and I do not run alone. That vast audience of family, friends, and leaders will cheer our courage, will applaud our determination as we rise from our stumblings and pursue our goal.

CAST OUT DOUBT

*Your faith should not stand in the
wisdom of men, but in the power of God.*

1 CORINTHIANS 2:5

Remember, faith and doubt cannot exist in the mind at the same time, for one will dispel the other. Cast out doubt. Cultivate faith. Strive always to retain that childlike faith which can move mountains and bring heaven closer to heart and home.

FEBRUARY

This is my commandment,
That ye love one another,
as I have loved you.

John 15:12

PROGRESS

Talk no more so exceeding proudly; let not arrogancy come out of your mouth: for the Lord is a God of knowledge, and by him actions are weighed.

1 SAMUEL 2:3

To meet the combined demands of the accumulated past and of the accumulating future, all of us need:

To act—not just react.

To innovate—not just imitate.

To program—not just protest.

To perform—not just proclaim.

To solve—not just resolve.

To accelerate—not just vacillate.

AN ECONOMIC LAW

*The hand of the diligent shall bear rule:
but the slothful shall be under tribute.*

PROVERBS 12:24

One cannot continually spend more than he earns and remain solvent. This law applies to nations as well as to men. A worker cannot, in the long run, adhere to a philosophy of something for nothing as opposed to something for something. Nor can management dismiss as optional the necessity of an adequate corporate profit and a reasonable return to shareholders if our economy of free enterprise is to flourish.

MORE THAN A TEACHER

I am the light and the life of the world.
I am Alpha and Omega, the beginning and the end.

3 Nephi 9:18

Of Him who delivered each of us from endless death, even Jesus Christ, I testify that He is a teacher of truth—but He is more than a teacher. He is the Exemplar of the perfect life—but He is more than an exemplar. He is the Great Physician—but He is more than a physician. He who rescued the "lost battalion" of mankind is the literal Savior of the world, the Son of God, the Prince of Peace, the Holy One of Israel—even the risen Lord—who declared, "I am the first and the last; I am he who liveth, I am he who was slain; I am your advocate with the Father" (D&C 110:4).

THREE KEYS TO SAFETY AND PEACE

He who doeth the works of righteousness
shall receive his reward, even peace in this world,
and eternal life in the world to come.

DOCTRINE AND COVENANTS 59:23

We live in a troubled world, a world of many challenges. We are here on this earth to deal with our individual challenges to the best of our ability, to learn from them, and to overcome them. Endure to the end we must, for our goal is eternal life in the presence of our Father in Heaven. He loves us and wants nothing more than for us to succeed in this goal. He will help us and bless us as we call upon Him in our prayers, as we study His words, and as we obey His commandments. Therein is found safety; therein is found peace.

SEEK THE BEST

*To some is given one, and to some is
given another, that all may be profited thereby.*

DOCTRINE AND COVENANTS 46:12

There are factors within you and within me,
even basic principles with which we have been
imbued from our creation, which seem to call
out and demand of us our best. Those particular yearnings and those cravings and those bits
of inspiration seem to be telling you and me,
"Seek the best in life. Look for opportunities
where you can be of greatest service."

A PRICELESS GIFT

There were many who were ordained and became high priests of God; and it was on account of their exceeding faith and repentance, and their righteousness before God, they choosing to repent and work righteousness rather than to perish.

ALMA 13:10

The gift of the priesthood is priceless. It carries with it the authority to act as God's servants, to administer to the sick, to bless our families, and to bless others as well. Its authority can reach beyond the veil of death, on into the eternities. There is nothing else to compare with it in all this world. Safeguard it, treasure it, live worthy of it.

ONLY FORGIVENESS HEALS

And now, the plan of mercy could not be brought about except an atonement should be made; therefore God himself atoneth for the sins of the world, to bring about the plan of mercy, to appease the demands of justice.

ALMA 42:15

From the springboard of such knowledge we ask ourselves, *Why, then, do we see on every side those instances where people decline to forgive one another and show forth the cleansing act of mercy and forgiveness? What blocks the way for such healing balm to cleanse human wounds? Is it stubbornness? Could it be pride? Maybe hatred has yet to melt and disappear.* "Blame keeps wounds open. Only forgiveness heals!" (from *O Pioneers!* by Willa Cather).

GOD-GIVEN INSTRUMENTS

Neglect not the gift that is in thee.

1 Timothy 4:14

Your training, your experience, your knowledge are tools to be skillfully used. They have been self-acquired. Your conscience, your love, and your faith are delicate and precious instruments to guide your destiny. They have been God-given.

WORTH EVERY EFFORT

Now ye have consecrated yourselves unto the Lord, come near and bring sacrifices and thank offerings into the house of the Lord.

2 CHRONICLES 29:31

Some degree of sacrifice has ever been associated with temple building and with temple attendance. Countless are those who have labored and struggled in order to obtain for themselves and for their families the blessings which are found in the temples of God.

Why are so many willing to give so much in order to receive the blessings of the temple? They understand that the saving ordinances received in the temple that permit us to someday return to our Heavenly Father in an eternal family relationship and to be endowed with blessings and power from on high are worth every sacrifice and every effort.

CHOOSE TO
FIND JOY

Happy are thy men, happy are these
thy servants, which stand continually before
thee, and that hear thy wisdom.

1 KINGS 10:8

We all know people who seem to "roll with the punches" so to speak, who are pleasant and cheerful through almost any challenge. Generally these are the people with whom we like to spend our time, for they make us feel better about circumstances and about ourselves. It seems that good things gravitate to them, for they don't let less-than-ideal circumstances stand in their way. They choose to find joy everywhere and to leave it behind them when they go.

LIVE GREATLY

Ye are of God, little children, and have
overcome them: because greater is he that is
in you, than he that is in the world.

1 JOHN 4:4

To live greatly, we must develop the capacity to face trouble with courage, disappointment with cheerfulness, and triumph with humility. You ask, "How might we achieve these goals?" I answer, "By getting a true perspective of who we really are!" We are sons and daughters of a living God in whose image we have been created.

OUR MOST CHERISHED GOAL

But blessed are they who are faithful and endure, whether in life or in death, for they shall inherit eternal life.

DOCTRINE AND COVENANTS 50:5

In one of Christopher Marlowe's plays, *The Tragical History of Dr. Faustus,* there is portrayed an individual, Dr. Faustus, who chose to ignore God and follow the pathway of Satan. At the end of his wicked life, and facing the frustration of opportunities lost and punishment certain to come, he lamented, "[There is] more searing anguish than [flaming] fire—eternal exile from God."

Just as eternal exile from God may be the most searing anguish, so eternal life in the presence of God is our most cherished goal.

THE DANGERS OF COMPLACENCY

At that day shall [the devil] . . . lull them away
into carnal security, that they will say: All is
well in Zion; yea, Zion prospereth, all is well—
and thus the devil cheateth their souls.

2 NEPHI 28:20–21

We cannot afford to be complacent. We live in perilous times; the signs are all around us. We are acutely aware of the negative influences in our society that stalk traditional families. At times television and movies portray worldly and immoral heroes and heroines and attempt to hold up as role models some actors and actresses whose lives are anything but exemplary. Why should we follow a blind guide?

We, as members of The Church of Jesus Christ of Latter-day Saints, must stand up to the dangers which surround us and our families.

SHOWING OUR LOVE

We love him, because he first loved us.

1 JOHN 4:19

The importance of demonstrating daily a true and an abiding love was convincingly taught by the Master when the inquiring lawyer stepped forward and boldly asked Him, "Master, which is the great commandment in the law?"

Matthew records that "Jesus said unto him, Thou shalt love the Lord thy God with all thy heart, and with all thy soul, and with all thy mind.

"This is the first and great commandment.

"And the second is like unto it, Thou shalt love thy neighbour as thyself" (Matthew 22:36–39).

FEET FIRMLY PLANTED

*Therefore, fear not, little flock; do good;
let earth and hell combine against you, for if ye
are built upon my rock, they cannot prevail.*

DOCTRINE AND COVENANTS 6:34

Occasionally discouragement may darken our pathway; frustration may be a constant companion. In our ears there may sound the sophistry of Satan as he whispers, "You cannot save the world; your efforts are meaningless. You haven't time to be concerned for others." Trusting in the Lord, let us turn our heads from such falsehoods and make certain our feet are firmly planted in the path of service and our hearts and souls dedicated to follow the example of the Lord.

ACHIEVING SELF-CONTROL

Use boldness, but not overbearance; and also see that ye bridle all your passions, that ye may be filled with love; see that ye refrain from idleness.

ALMA 38:12

In our science-oriented age, we conquer space but cannot control self; hence, we forfeit peace.

Through modern science, man has been permitted to fly through space at great speeds and to silently and without effort cruise sixty days under water in nuclear-powered ships. Now that man can fly like a bird and swim like a fish, would that he could learn to walk on earth like a man.

MODERN
PIED PIPERS

Behold, verily I say unto you, that there are
many spirits which are false spirits, which have
gone forth in the earth, deceiving the world.

DOCTRINE AND COVENANTS 50:2

Do you, with me, remember the story from childhood days of that persuasive musician, the Pied Piper of Hamelin? Are there Pied Pipers even today? Are they playing alluring music to lead, to their own destruction, those who listen and follow? These "pipers" pipe the tunes of *pride* and *pleasure*, of *selfishness* and *greed* and leave in their wake confused minds, troubled hearts, empty lives, and destroyed dreams.

The world is in need of your help. There are feet to steady, hands to grasp, minds to encourage, hearts to inspire, and souls to save.

EXTENDING HELP AND HOPE

Think of your brethren like unto yourselves, and be familiar with all and free with your substance, that they may be rich like unto you.

JACOB 2:17

We have a responsibility to extend help as well as hope to the hungry, to the homeless, and to the downtrodden both at home and abroad. Such assistance is being provided for the blessing of all. In a host of cities, where need has outdistanced help, lives have been lifted, hearts have been touched, and the frown of despair has been transformed to the smile of confidence, thanks to the generosity of the Church membership in the payment of their fast offerings as the Lord has commanded.

A SACRED CALL

And if they desire to take upon them my name with
full purpose of heart, they are called to go into all the
world to preach my gospel unto every creature.

DOCTRINE AND COVENANTS 18:28

Our missionaries are not salesmen with wares to peddle; rather, they are servants of the Most High God, with testimonies to bear, truths to teach, and souls to save.

Each missionary who goes forth in response to a sacred call becomes a servant of the Lord whose work this truly is.

Your Own "Sacred Grove"

Yea, humble yourselves, and continue in prayer unto him.
Cry unto him when ye are in your fields, yea, over
all your flocks. Cry unto him in your houses, yea, over all
your household, both morning, mid-day, and evening.

Alma 34:19–21

The boy prophet Joseph Smith sought heavenly help by entering a grove which then became sacred. Do we need similar strength? Does each need to seek his or her own "Sacred Grove"? A place where communion between God and man can go forth unimpeded, uninterrupted, and undisturbed is such a grove.

THE WORDS WE SAY

Be thou an example of the believers,
in word, in conversation, in charity,
in spirit, in faith, in purity.

1 TIMOTHY 4:12

What we say and how we say it tend to reflect what we are. In the life of the Apostle Peter, when he attempted to distance himself from Jesus and pretended to be other than what he was, his tormenters detected his true identity with the penetrating statement, "Thy speech [betrayeth] thee" (Matthew 26:73). The words we utter will reflect the feelings of our hearts, the strength of our character, and the depth of our testimonies.

SAIL ON

And it came to pass that I, Nephi,
did guide the ship, that we sailed again
towards the promised land.

1 NEPHI 18:22

Beware of the flashy start and the fade-out finish.

Follow the example of Christopher Columbus. Take a leaf out of the log of his journal on his first voyage. Day after day, as they hoped to find land and never found it, he wrote simply, "This day we sailed on."

THE WAY
TO SUCCESS

Wealth gotten by vanity shall be diminished:
but he that gathereth by labour shall increase.

PROVERBS 13:11

The best way to prepare for your future does not consist of merely dreaming about it. Great men and women have not been merely dreamers; they have returned from their visions to the practicalities of replacing the airy stones of the dream castles with solid masonry wrought by their hands. Vision without work is daydreaming. Work without vision is drudgery. Vision, coupled with work, will ensure your success.

CHOOSING YOUR PATH

And then are ye in this strait and narrow path which leads to eternal life; yea, ye have entered in by the gate; ye have done according to the commandments of the Father and the Son; and ye have received the Holy Ghost.

2 NEPHI 31:18

Let us not find ourselves as indecisive as is Alice in Lewis Carroll's classic *Alice's Adventures in Wonderland*. You will remember that she comes to a crossroads with two paths before her, each stretching onward but in opposite directions. She is confronted by the Cheshire cat, of whom Alice asks, "Which path shall I follow?"

The cat answers, "That depends where you want to go. If you do not know where you want to go, it doesn't matter which path you take."

Unlike Alice, we all know where we want to go, and it *does* matter which way we go, for by choosing our path, we choose our destination.

FILL YOUR HOMES WITH LOVE

And this commandment have we from him,
That he who loveth God love his brother also.

1 JOHN 4:21

May your homes be filled with love and courtesy and with the Spirit of the Lord. Love your families. If there are disagreements or contentions among you, I urge you to settle them now.

GUIDED BY YOUR CONSCIENCE

These are they that are redeemed of the Lord; yea, these are they that are taken out, that are delivered from that endless night of darkness; and thus they stand or fall; for behold, they are their own judges, whether to do good or do evil.

ALMA 41:7

Doing what's right is the easiest thing to judge of all. Whenever you're about to do something and that little voice in your head stops you and asks the question, "Should I?" the chances are you shouldn't. We all have a conscience, and it's there for a purpose. We should always be guided by it, rather than running from it.

A COMPASS FOR OUR LIVES

For all who will have a blessing at my hands shall abide the law which was appointed for that blessing, and the conditions thereof, as were instituted from before the foundation of the world.

DOCTRINE AND COVENANTS 132:5

The holy endowment that we receive in our temples can well be the compass for our lives. Our course, our eternal course, is charted by the scriptures; and the voice that has come and continues to come from the heavens to God's prophets and in answer to humble, personal, and family prayer will ever guide us back to our eternal home. We need but to do our part. However, that ancient principle is still true that nothing can be had for nothing. All blessings are predicated on obedience to law.

THE GIFT OF LOVE

But in all things approving ourselves as the ministers
of God, in much patience, in afflictions, in necessities, in
distresses, . . . By pureness, by knowledge, by longsuffering,
by kindness, by the Holy Ghost, by love unfeigned.

2 CORINTHIANS 6:4, 6

A segment of our society desperately yearning for an expression of true love is found among those growing older, and particularly when they suffer from pangs of loneliness. The chill wind of dying hopes and vanished dreams whistles through the ranks of the elderly and those who approach the declining side of the summit of life. "What they need in the loneliness of their older years is . . . what we needed in the uncertain years of our youth: a sense of belonging, an assurance of being wanted, and the kindly ministrations of loving hearts and hands" (*Thoughts . . . for One Hundred Days*, 222). So wrote Elder Richard L. Evans some years ago.

MARCH

*For after much tribulation come
the blessings. Wherefore the day cometh
that ye shall be crowned with much glory;
the hour is not yet, but is nigh at hand.*

DOCTRINE AND COVENANTS 58:4

PRIZED POSSESSIONS

And upon these I write the things of my soul, and many of the scriptures which are engraven upon the plates of brass. For my soul delighteth in the scriptures, and my heart pondereth them, and writeth them for the learning and the profit of my children.

2 NEPHI 4:15

The words of truth and inspiration found in our four standard works are prized possessions to me. I never tire of reading them. I am lifted spiritually whenever I search the scriptures. These holy words of truth and love give guidance to my life and point the way to eternal perfection.

THE PEACE OF GOD

The Lord our God did visit us with assurances
that he would deliver us; yea, insomuch that he did speak
peace to our souls, and did grant unto us great faith, and did
cause us that we should hope for our deliverance in him.

ALMA 58:11

The famed statesman William Gladstone described the formula for peace when he declared: "We look forward to the time when the power of love will replace the love of power. Then will our world know the blessings of peace."

World peace, though a lofty goal, is but an outgrowth of the personal peace each individual seeks to attain. I refer not to the peace promoted by man, but peace as promised of God. I speak of peace in our homes, peace in our hearts, even peace in our lives. Peace after the way of man is perishable. Peace after the manner of God will prevail.

FROM SINNER TO SAINT

And immediately there fell from his eyes
as it had been scales: and he received sight
forthwith, and arose, and was baptized.

ACTS 9:18

Following the earthly ministry of the Lord, there were many who, rather than deny their testimony of Him, would forfeit their lives. Such was Paul the apostle. The impulse of his father to send him to Jerusalem opened the door to Paul's destiny. He would pass through it and help to shape a new world.

Gifted in his capacity to stir, move, and manage groups of men, Paul was a peerless example of one who nobly made the transition from sinner to saint. Though disappointment, heartache, and trial were to beset him, yet Paul, at the conclusion of his ministry, could say, "I have kept the faith" (2 Timothy 4:7).

WORTHY TO REPRESENT THE LORD

*There has been a day of calling,
but the time has come for a day of choosing;
and let those be chosen that are worthy.*

DOCTRINE AND COVENANTS 105:35

Prepare for service as a missionary. Keep yourselves clean and pure and worthy to represent the Lord. Maintain your health and strength. Study the scriptures.

To those of you who are not yet to the season of life when you might serve a couples mission, I urge you to prepare now for the day when you and your spouse might do so. As your circumstances allow, make yourselves available to leave home and give full-time missionary service. There are few times in your lives when you will enjoy the sweet spirit and satisfaction that come from giving full-time service together in the work of the Master.

A HOUSE
OF LEARNING

*For now have I chosen and sanctified this house,
that my name may be there for ever: and mine eyes
and mine heart shall be there perpetually.*

2 CHRONICLES 7:16

As I think of temples, my thoughts turn to the many blessings we receive therein. As we enter through the doors of the temple, we leave behind us the distractions and confusion of the world. Inside this sacred sanctuary, we find beauty and order. There is rest for our souls and a respite from the cares of our lives.

As we attend the temple, there can come to us a dimension of spirituality and a feeling of peace which will transcend any other feeling which could come into the human heart.

THE ENEMY
OF ACHIEVEMENT

Yea, I know that I am nothing;
as to my strength I am weak; therefore I will
not boast of myself, but I will boast of my God,
for in his strength I can do all things.

ALMA 26:12

As you define your goals and plan for their achievement, ponder the thought: The past is behind—learn from it; the future is ahead—prepare for it; the present is here —live in it.

At times, all of us let that enemy of achievement—even the culprit, self-defeat—dwarf our aspirations, smother our dreams, cloud our vision, and wreck our lives. The enemy's voice whispers in our ears, "I can't do it." "I'm too little." "Everyone is watching." "I'm nobody." This is when we need to reflect on the counsel of Maxwell Maltz, who declared: "The most realistic self-image of all is to conceive of yourself as made in the image of God."

THE LUXURY
WE CAN'T AFFORD

*And it came to pass that many
were drowned in the depths of the fountain;
and many were lost from his view,
wandering in strange roads.*

1 NEPHI 8:32

We must not detour from our determined course. In our journey we will encounter forks and turnings in the road. There will be the inevitable trials of our faith and temptations of our times. We simply cannot afford the luxury of a detour, for certain detours lead to destruction and spiritual death. Let us avoid the moral quicksands that threaten on every side, the whirlpools of sin, and the crosscurrents of uninspired philosophies.

WE CANNOT STAND STILL

He gave commandments unto men, they having first trans-gressed the first commandments as to things which were tem-poral, and becoming as gods, knowing good from evil, placing themselves in a state to act, or being placed in a state to act.

ALMA 12:31

Time is the raw material of life. Every day unwraps itself like a gift, bringing us the opportunity to spin a fabric of health, pleasure, and content, and to evolve into something better than we are at its beginning.

Every passing instant is a juncture of many roads open to our choice. Shall we do this or that? Go this way or that? We cannot stand still. Choosing between alternatives in the use of time is evidence of one of the noblest of God's gifts—freedom of choice.

GIVING AND RECEIVING

As every man hath received the gift,
even so minister the same one to another, as good
stewards of the manifold grace of God.

1 PETER 4:10

I have shewed you all things, how that so labouring ye ought to support the weak, and to remember the words of the Lord Jesus, how he said, It is more blessed to give than to receive" (Acts 20:35). This is a truth more profound than most of us realize. Furthermore, it is a very practical truth. Many of the problems of our times arise out of an excess of receiving.

PRAY IN YOUR FAMILIES

*Pray in your families unto the Father,
always in my name, that your wives and
your children may be blessed.*

3 NEPHI 18:21

As we offer unto the Lord our family and our personal prayers, let us do so with faith and trust in Him. Let us remember the injunction of Paul to the Hebrews: "For he that cometh to God must believe that he is, and that he is a rewarder of them that diligently seek him" (Hebrews 11:6).

THE ULTIMATE LIBRARY

*And as all have not faith, seek ye diligently
and teach one another words of wisdom; yea, seek
ye out of the best books words of wisdom, seek
learning even by study and also by faith.*

DOCTRINE AND COVENANTS 109:7

James A. Michener, prominent author, suggests: "A nation becomes what its young people read in their youth. Its ideals are fashioned then, its goals strongly determined."

The Lord counseled, "Seek ye out of the best books words of wisdom; seek learning, even by study and also by faith" (D&C 88:118).

Of course, the standard works offer the ultimate library of learning of which I speak. Let us read from them often, that we may be enlightened and edified and draw closer to the Lord.

A VISION OF OUR OPPORTUNITY

*I will also give thee for a light
to the Gentiles, that thou mayest be my
salvation unto the end of the earth.*

ISAIAH 49:6

There are millions of people yet to hear the message of the Restoration, and we must not say *no* in their behalf. We cannot judge whom the Lord may prepare to hear His message. Some we may least expect are ones who are best prepared to accept the gospel. What is needed by you and me? A vision of our opportunity. And then a desire to really be a neighbor.

EQUAL TO
OUR CHALLENGES

*The power and authority of the higher,
or Melchizedek Priesthood, is to hold the keys
of all the spiritual blessings of the church.*

DOCTRINE AND COVENANTS 107:18

All who hold the priesthood have opportunities for service to our Heavenly Father and to His children here on earth. It is contrary to the spirit of service to live selfishly within ourselves and disregard the needs of others. The Lord will guide us and make us equal to the challenges before us.

ORDER IN THE CHURCH

Behold, mine house is a house of order, saith the Lord God, and not a house of confusion.

DOCTRINE AND COVENANTS 132:8

We do not appoint ourselves to the positions we occupy; there is order in the Church. Calls to serve come through that priesthood channel as established by our Heavenly Father. When we remember this, we can then appreciate that we are on the Lord's errand and thus entitled to His divine help. We can, with effectiveness, serve God and serve our fellowmen.

A Call
for Help

Teach them to never be weary of
good works, but to be meek and lowly in heart;
for such shall find rest to their souls.

ALMA 37:34

Today there are hearts to gladden, there are deeds to be done—even precious souls to save. The sick, the weary, the hungry, the cold, the injured, the lonely, the aged, the wanderer—all cry out for our help.

The road signs of life enticingly invite every traveler: This way to fame; this way to affluence; this way to popularity; this way to luxury. Pause at the crossroads before you continue your journey. Listen for that still, small voice which ever so gently beckons, "Come, follow me."

OUR MAJOR CHALLENGE

*And now I say unto you, all you that are
desirous to follow the voice of the good shepherd,
come ye out from the wicked, and be ye separate,
and touch not their unclean things.*

ALMA 5:57

As we travel throughout the world, very often
the members of the Church, and particularly the
priesthood leaders, ask us, "What do you consider the greatest problem facing the Church?"
I usually answer, "Our major challenge for the
membership of the Church is to live in the world
without being of the world." I would like to emphasize that in this day in which we live, the
floodwaters of immorality, irresponsibility, and
dishonesty lap at the very moorings of our individual lives. If we do not safeguard those moorings, if we do not have deeply entrenched foun-
dations to withstand such eroding influences, we
are going to be in difficulty.

SEEK THE SPIRIT

Who also hath made us able ministers of
the new testament; not of the letter, but of the spirit:
for the letter killeth, but the spirit giveth life.

2 CORINTHIANS 3:6

The Apostle Paul, in his second epistle to the Corinthians, urges that we turn from the narrow confinement of the letter of the law and seek the open vista of opportunity which the Spirit provides. I love and cherish Paul's statement: "The letter killeth, but the spirit giveth life" (2 Corinthians 3:6).

In a day of danger or a time of trial, such knowledge, such hope, such understanding bring comfort to the troubled mind and grieving heart. The feeling of being lost in the crowd of life vanishes with the certain knowledge that our Heavenly Father is mindful of each of us.

ATTITUDE MAKES ALL THE DIFFERENCE

*Search diligently, pray always, and
be believing, and all things shall work together for
your good, if ye walk uprightly and remember the covenant
wherewith ye have covenanted one with another.*

DOCTRINE AND COVENANTS 90:24

Attitude can make all the difference in our lives, and we control our attitude. It can make us miserable or happy, content or dissatisfied. To a great degree, it can make us strong or weak.

ENTITLED TO
THE LORD'S HELP

With whom my hand shall be established:
mine arm also shall strengthen him.

PSALM 89:21

Our task is not insurmountable. We are on the Lord's errand, and therefore we are entitled to the Lord's help. But we must try. From the stage play *Shenandoah* comes the spoken line which inspires: "If we don't try, then we don't do; and if we don't do, then why are we here?"

When the Master ministered among men, He called fishermen at Galilee to leave their nets and follow Him, declaring, "I will make you fishers of men" (Matthew 4:19). And so He did. Tonight He issues a call to each of us to "come join the ranks" ("We Are All Enlisted," *Hymns*, no. 250).

FAMILY PRAYER

Therefore, hold up your light that it may shine unto the world. Behold I am the light which ye shall hold up— that which ye have seen me do. Behold ye see that I have prayed unto the Father, and ye all have witnessed.

3 NEPHI 18:24

A prominent American judge was asked what we as citizens of the countries of the world could do to reduce crime and disobedience to law and to bring peace and contentment into our lives and into our nations. He carefully replied, "I would suggest a return to the old-fashioned practice of family prayer."

As a people, aren't we grateful that family prayer is not an out-of-date practice with us? There is no more beautiful sight in all this world than to see a family praying together. The oft-repeated phrase is ever true, "The family that prays together stays together."

A LIFETIME
OF RIGHTEOUSNESS

*And, if you keep my commandments
and endure to the end you shall have eternal life,
which gift is the greatest of all the gifts of God.*

DOCTRINE AND COVENANTS 14:7

Eternal life in the kingdom of our Father is your goal.

Such a goal is not achieved in one glorious attempt, but rather is the result of a lifetime of righteousness, an accumulation of wise choices, even a constancy of purpose. Like the coveted "A" grade on the report card of a difficult and required college course, the reward of eternal life requires effort.

AN ATTITUDE
OF LOVE

Beloved, let us love one another:
for love is of God; and every one that loveth
is born of God, and knoweth God.

1 JOHN 4:7

Finally, there is the Attitude of Love. Such an attitude characterized the mission of the Master. He gave sight to the blind, legs to the lame, and life to the dead. Perhaps when we face our Maker, we will not be asked, "How many positions did you hold?" but rather, "How many people did you help?" In reality, you can never love the Lord until you serve Him by serving His people.

FINDING PEACE

Peace I leave with you, my peace I give unto you: not as the world giveth, give I unto you. Let not your heart be troubled, neither let it be afraid.

JOHN 14:27

In a world where peace is such a universal quest, we sometimes wonder why violence walks our streets, accounts of murder and senseless killings fill the columns of our newspapers, and family quarrels and disputes mar the sanctity of the home and smother the tranquility of so many lives.

Perhaps we stray from the path which leads to peace and find it necessary to pause, to ponder, and to reflect on the teachings of the Prince of Peace and determine to incorporate them in our thoughts and actions and to live a higher law, walk a more elevated road, and be a better disciple of Christ.

A DESIGN
AND A DESIGNER

Ye cannot behold with your natural eyes, for the present time, the design of your God concerning those things which shall come hereafter, and the glory which shall follow after much tribulation.

DOCTRINE AND COVENANTS 58:3

If there is a design in this world in which we live, there must be a Designer. Who can behold the many wonders of the universe without believing that there is a design for all mankind? Who can doubt that there is a Designer?

Missionary Service

*But purify your hearts before me; and then
go ye into all the world, and preach my gospel
unto every creature who has not received it.*

Doctrine and Covenants 112:28

Prepare to serve worthily, with an eye single to the glory of God and His purposes. You will never know the full influence of your testimony and your service, but you will return with gladness for having had the privilege of responding to a sacred call to serve the Master. You will be forever loved by those to whom you bring the light of truth. Your teachings will be found in their service. Your examples will be guides to follow. Your faith will prompt courage to meet life's challenges.

PRAY DAILY

*Pray always, and I will pour out my Spirit
upon you, and great shall be your blessing—yea, even
more than if you should obtain treasures of earth.*

DOCTRINE AND COVENANTS 19:38

Our journey into the future will not be a smooth highway which stretches from here to eternity. Rather, there will be forks and turnings in the road, to say nothing of the unanticipated bumps. We must pray daily to a loving Heavenly Father, who wants each of us to succeed in life.

RESCUERS NEEDED

And now, as ye have begun to teach the word even
so I would that ye should continue to teach; and I would
that ye would be diligent and temperate in all things.

ALMA 38:10

For Latter-day Saints, the need to rescue our brothers and sisters who have, for one reason or another, strayed from the path of Church activity is of eternal significance. Do we know of such people who once embraced the gospel? If so, what is our responsibility to rescue them?

Some struggle with sin, while others wander in fear or apathy or ignorance. For whatever reason, they have isolated themselves from activity in the Church. And they will almost certainly remain lost unless there awakens in us—the active members of the Church—a desire to rescue and to save.

POWERS EQUAL TO YOUR TASKS

I know both how to be abased, and I know how to abound:
every where and in all things I am instructed both to be
full and to be hungry, both to abound and to suffer need.
I can do all things through Christ which strengtheneth me.

PHILIPPIANS 4:12–13

Oh, do not pray for tasks equal to your powers. Pray for powers equal to your tasks. Then the doing of your work shall be no miracle, but you shall be the miracle.

Your Heavenly Father will not leave you to struggle along, but stands ever ready to help. Most often such assistance comes quietly, at other times with dramatic impact.

Our Purpose

*And behold, **I** tell you these things*
that ye may learn wisdom; that ye may learn that
when ye are in the service of your fellow beings
ye are only in the service of your God.

Mosiah 2:17

No person can go to the temple for himself or for another without learning something. As we learn, we come to know, and when we come to know, we come to do, and that is our purpose—to serve our Heavenly Father and help others along the way.

CHANGING OUR VERY LIVES

And he said unto the children of men:
Follow thou me. Wherefore, my beloved brethren,
can we follow Jesus save we shall be willing
to keep the commandments of the Father?

2 NEPHI 31:10

The Master could be found mingling with the poor, the downtrodden, the oppressed, and the afflicted. He brought hope to the hopeless, strength to the weak, and freedom to the captive. He taught of the better life to come—even eternal life. This knowledge ever directs those who receive the divine injunction: "Follow thou me." It guided Peter. It motivated Paul. It can determine our personal destiny. Can we make the decision to follow in righteousness and truth the Redeemer of the world? With His help a rebellious boy can become an obedient man, a wayward girl can cast aside the old self and begin anew.

A PRECARIOUS JOURNEY

Wherefore, men are free according to the flesh; and all things are given them which are expedient unto man. And they are free to choose liberty and eternal life, through the great Mediator of all men, or to choose captivity and death.

2 NEPHI 2:27

We who chose the Savior's plan knew that we would be embarking on a precarious, difficult journey, for we walk the ways of the world and sin and stumble, cutting us off from our Father. But the Firstborn in the Spirit offered Himself as a sacrifice to atone for the sins of all. Through unspeakable suffering He became the great Redeemer, the Savior of all mankind, thus making possible our successful return to our Father.

APRIL

Jesus said unto her, I am the resurrection,
and the life: he that believeth in me, though
he were dead, yet shall he live: And whosoever
liveth and believeth in me shall never die.

<small>JOHN 11:25–26</small>

WHEN BOUNDARIES ARE STRETCHED

Better is the poor that walketh in
his integrity, than he that is perverse
in his lips, and is a fool.

PROVERBS 19:1

We have observed in recent years the accelerating erosion of many of the restraints upon human conduct which have guided the lives of past generations. Theology has stretched its boundaries to embrace thinkers who proclaim the death of God, and God's orphans are freed to indulge their selfishness according to their whims.

There are those who declare chastity to be a state of mind rather than a physical condition. Integrity, which was once a fixed and absolute quality, has taken on a new flexibility. Our intellectual and moral condition has fallen hopelessly behind our technical progress. You can help restore the balance.

PREPARE FOR THE FUTURE

*Prepare ye, prepare ye
for that which is to come,
for the Lord is nigh.*

DOCTRINE AND COVENANTS 1:12

We live in a changing world. Technology has altered nearly every aspect of our lives. We must cope with these advances—even these cataclysmic changes—in a world of which our forebears never dreamed.

Remember the promise of the Lord: "If ye are prepared ye shall not fear" (D&C 38:30). Fear is a deadly enemy of progress.

It is necessary to prepare and to plan so that we don't fritter away our lives. Without a goal, there can be no real success.

THINK TO THANK

*Enter into his gates with thanksgiving,
and into his courts with praise: be thankful
unto him, and bless him name.*

PSALM 100:4

Think to thank. In these three words you
have the finest capsule course for a happy marriage, the formula for enduring friendships,
and a pattern for personal happiness.

A Power Stronger than Weapons

And again, he that trembleth under my power shall be made strong, and shall bring forth fruits of praise and wisdom, according to the revelations and truths which I have given you.

Doctrine and Covenants 52:17

Many have heavy crosses to bear. With the birth of the Babe in Bethlehem, there emerged a great endowment—a power stronger than weapons, a wealth more lasting than coins. He may come to us as one unknown, without a name, as by the lakeside He came to those men who knew Him not. He speaks to us the same words, "Follow thou me," and sets us to the task which He has to fulfill for our time. He commands, and to those who obey Him, whether they be wise or simple, He will reveal Himself in the toils, the conflicts, the sufferings that they shall pass through in His fellowship; and they shall learn in their own experience who He is.

THE MASTER'S PROMISE OF PEACE

These things I have spoken unto you, that in me ye might have peace. In the world ye shall have tribulation: but be of good cheer; I have overcome the world.

JOHN 16:33

Frequently, death comes as an intruder. Death lays its heavy hand upon those dear to us and leaves us baffled and wondering. The Master's promise of peace is a comforting balm: "Peace I leave with you, my peace I give unto you: not as the world giveth, give I unto you. Let not your heart be troubled, neither let it be afraid" (John 14:27). "I go to prepare a place for you . . . ; that where I am, there ye may be also" (John 14:2–3).

How I pray that all who have loved then lost might know the reality of the Resurrection and have the unshakable knowledge that families can be forever.

SEARCHING FOR TRUTH

And that which doth not edify is not of God, and is darkness. That which is of God is light; and he that receiveth light, and continueth in God, receiveth more light; and that light groweth brighter and brighter until the perfect day.

DOCTRINE AND COVENANTS 50:23–24

You do not find truth groveling through error. Truth is found by searching, studying, and living the revealed word of God. We learn truth when we associate with truth. We adopt error when we mingle with error.

The Lord instructed us concerning how we might distinguish between truth and error when He said: "That which doth not edify is not of God, and is darkness. That which is of God is light."

A NEED FOR EVERY ONE

That the fulness of my gospel might be proclaimed by the weak and the simple unto the ends of the world, and before kings and rulers.

DOCTRINE AND COVENANTS 1:23

Let there be no mistake—there is a need for every one of us to be a missionary. Our Lord and Savior has endowed you and me with certain abilities and characteristics. He has made it possible for some missionaries to appeal to certain men, others to appeal to another group. Every child of God is needed in this great missionary cause.

THE POWER OF GOD

O the greatness and the justice of our God!
For he executeth all his words, and they have gone forth
out of his mouth, and his law must be fulfilled.

2 Nephi 9:17

Miracles are everywhere to be found when the priesthood is understood, its power is honored and used properly, and faith is exerted. When faith replaces doubt, when selfless service eliminates selfish striving, the power of God brings to pass His purposes.

THE WAY OF
THE LORD

And see that ye have faith, hope, and charity,
and then ye will always abound in good works.

ALMA 7:24

No member of The Church of Jesus Christ of Latter-day Saints who has canned peas, topped beets, hauled hay, shoveled coal, or helped in any way to serve others ever forgets or regrets the experience of helping provide for those in need. Devoted men and women help to operate this vast and inspired welfare program. In reality, the plan would never succeed on effort alone, for this program operates through faith after the way of the Lord.

A CHANNEL
OF TRUTH

*If thou shalt ask, thou shalt receive revelation upon
revelation, knowledge upon knowledge, that thou
mayest know the mysteries and peaceable things—that
which bringeth joy, that which bringeth life eternal.*

DOCTRINE AND COVENANTS 42:61

How grateful we should be that revelation,
the clear and uncluttered channel of truth, is
still open. Our Heavenly Father continues to
inspire His prophets. This inspiration can serve
as a sure guide in making life's decisions. It will
lead us to truth.

SEEK HIM IN SIMPLE THINGS

And now, my beloved brethren, I know by this that unless a man shall endure to the end, in following the example of the Son of the living God, he cannot be saved.

2 NEPHI 31:16

How do we find the Lord? I believe we have to seek Him in simple things. I believe we have to seek Him in personal prayer. I believe we must seek Him in personal service. I believe we seek and find Jesus when we follow His example.

KEEPING AHEAD
OF CHANGE

*Shall we not go on in so great a cause? Go forward
and not backward. Courage, brethren; and on, on to the
victory! Let your hearts rejoice, and be exceedingly glad.*

DOCTRINE AND COVENANTS 128:22

While we reach outward, we have the responsibility to press onward. Whatever part you choose to play on the world stage, keep in mind that life is like a candid camera; it does not wait for you to pose. Learning how to direct our resources wisely is a high priority. We don't have to keep up with the change. We have to keep ahead of it.

THE LORD IS ON OUR SIDE

Men are, that they might have joy.

2 NEPHI 2:25

Let us be of good cheer as we go about our lives. Although we live in increasingly perilous times, the Lord loves us and is mindful of us. He is always on our side as we do what is right. He will help us in time of need. Difficulties come into our lives, problems we do not anticipate and which we would never choose. None of us is immune. The purpose of mortality is to learn and to grow to be more like our Father, and it is often during the difficult times that we learn the most, as painful as the lessons may be. Our lives can also be filled with joy as we follow the teachings of the gospel of Jesus Christ.

GIVE OUR LIVES IN SERVICE

The Son of Man hath descended below them all. Art thou greater than he?

DOCTRINE AND COVENANTS 122:8

As we move toward the future, we must not neglect the lessons of the past. Our Heavenly Father gave His Son. The Son of God gave His life. We are asked by Them to give our lives, as it were, in Their divine service. Will you? Will I? Will we? There are lessons to be taught, there are kind deeds to be done, there are souls to be saved.

Let us remember the counsel of King Benjamin: "When ye are in the service of your fellow beings ye are only in the service of your God" (Mosiah 2:17). Reach out to rescue those who need your help. Lift such to the higher road and the better way.

TRUE LOVE
CHANGES LIVES

Seeing ye have purified your souls in obeying the truth through the Spirit unto unfeigned love of the brethren, see that ye love one another with a pure heart fervently.

1 PETER 1:22

Some point the accusing finger at the sinner or the unfortunate and in derision say, "He has brought his condition upon himself." Others exclaim, "Oh, he will never change. He has always been a bad one." A few see beyond the outward appearance and recognize the true worth of a human soul. When they do, miracles occur. The downtrodden, the discouraged, the helpless become "no more strangers and foreigners, but fellow citizens with the saints, and of the household of God" (Ephesians 2:19). True love can alter human lives and change human nature.

An Open Heart

For they that are wise and have received the truth, and have taken the Holy Spirit for their guide, and have not been deceived—verily I say unto you, they shall not be hewn down and cast into the fire, but shall abide the day.

DOCTRINE AND COVENANTS 45:57

Be influenced by that still, small voice. Remember that one with authority placed his hands on your head at the time of your confirmation and said, "Receive the Holy Ghost." Open your hearts, even your very souls, to the sound of that special voice which testifies of truth.

A PATTERN OF PRAYER

*All victory and glory is brought to pass unto you through
your diligence, faithfulness, and prayers of faith.*

DOCTRINE AND COVENANTS 103:36

When we are weighed in the balances we will not be found wanting if we make personal prayer a pattern for our lives. When we remember that each of us is literally a spirit son or daughter of God, we will not find it difficult to approach our Father in Heaven.

A SOURCE OF STRENGTH AND KNOWLEDGE

He that keepeth [God's] commandments receiveth truth and light, until he is glorified in truth and knoweth all things.

DOCTRINE AND COVENANTS 93:28

A knowledge of truth and the answers to our greatest questions come to us as we are obedient to the commandments of God.

Obedience is a hallmark of prophets; it has provided strength and knowledge to them throughout the ages. We, as well, are entitled to this source of strength and knowledge. It is available to each of us as we obey God's commandments.

HIDDEN WEDGES

For verily, verily I say unto you, he that hath the spirit
of contention is not of me, but is of the devil, who is
the father of contention, and he stirreth up the hearts
of men to contend with anger, one with another.

3 NEPHI 11:29

Sometimes we can take offense so easily. On other occasions we are too stubborn to accept a sincere apology. Who will subordinate ego, pride, and hurt—then step forward with, "I am truly sorry! Let's be as we once were: friends. Let's not pass to future generations the grievances, the anger of our time"? Let's remove any hidden wedges that can do nothing but destroy.

Where do hidden wedges originate? Some come from unresolved disputes, which lead to ill feelings. Others find their beginnings in disappointments, jealousies, arguments, and imagined hurts. We must lay them to rest and not leave them to canker, fester, and ultimately destroy.

THE GIFT
OF PEACE

Wherefore, be of good cheer, and do not fear,
for I the Lord am with you, and will stand by you.

DOCTRINE AND COVENANTS 68:6

With the ancients we may wonder, "Is there no balm in Gilead?" (Jeremiah 8:22). There is a certain sadness, even hopelessness, in the verse:

There is never a life without sadness,
There is never a heart free from pain;
If one seeks in this world for true solace,
He seeks it forever in vain.

He who was burdened with sorrow and acquainted with grief speaks to every troubled heart and bestows the gift of peace. "Peace I leave with you, my peace I give unto you: not as the world giveth, give I unto you. Let not your heart be troubled, neither let it be afraid" (John 14:27).

IN SEARCH OF
OUR BEST SELVES

*Remember faith, virtue, knowledge,
temperance, patience, brotherly kindness,
godliness, charity, humility, diligence.*

DOCTRINE AND COVENANTS 4:6

In our mortal journey, the advice of the Apostle Paul provides heavenly guidance: "Whatsoever things are true, whatsoever things are honest, whatsoever things are just, whatsoever things are pure, whatsoever things are lovely, whatsoever things are of good report; if there be any virtue, and if there be any praise, think on these things" (Philippians 4:8).

In the search for our best selves, several questions will guide our thinking: Am I what I want to be? Am I closer to the Savior today than I was yesterday? Will I be closer yet tomorrow? Do I have the courage to change for the better?

"HEAVEN WOULD NOT BE HEAVEN"

I saw Father Adam and Abraham; and my father and my mother; my brother Alvin . . . ; and marveled how it was that he had obtained an inheritance in that kingdom.

DOCTRINE AND COVENANTS 137:5–6

An appreciation for the temple endowment and the sealing ordinances will bring the members of our families closer together, and there will be quickened within each family member a desire to make available these same blessings to our loved ones who have gone beyond. We will come to say with George Eliot, "I desire no future that would break the ties of the past, for heaven would not be heaven without family and friends."

PERSEVERE TOWARD THE GOAL

*Continue in the faith grounded and settled,
and be not moved away from the hope of the gospel.*

Colossians 1:23

We may find that there are times in our lives when we falter, when we become weary or fatigued, or when we suffer a disappointment or heartache. When that happens, I would hope that we will persevere with even greater effort toward our goal.

THE NEED FOR GOOD FRIENDS

Stand fast, and hold the traditions which ye have been taught, whether by word, or our epistle.

2 THESSALONIANS 2:15

We tend to become like those whom we admire. We adopt the mannerisms, the attitudes, even the conduct of those whom we admire—and they are usually our friends. Associate with those who, like you, are planning not for temporary convenience, shallow goals, or narrow ambition, but rather for those things that matter most—even eternal objectives.

A RULE
FOR SUCCESS

He which soweth sparingly shall reap also sparingly;
and he which soweth bountifully shall reap also bountifully.

2 CORINTHIANS 9:6

In professional, business, scientific, and technological life there is a rule which can be a very good rule for ambitious young persons. The rule is, "Find a vacuum and expand into it." Ask yourself, "What is there that needs doing and is not being done?" Then assess your capacity for doing things and let it be your ambition to do the work that you can do best, in an area where it is needed most, and then put all your mind into it.

GIVE THANKS

In every thing give thanks: for this is
the will of God in Christ Jesus concerning you.

1 THESSALONIANS 5:18

Do we remember to give thanks for the blessings we receive? Sincerely giving thanks not only helps us recognize our blessings, but it also unlocks the doors of heaven and helps us feel God's love.

My beloved friend President Gordon B. Hinckley said, "When you walk with gratitude, you do not walk with arrogance and conceit and egotism, you walk with a spirit of thanksgiving that is becoming to you and will bless your lives" (*Teachings of Gordon B. Hinckley* [1997], 250).

MUCH MORE THAN A HOUSE

See that they are more diligent
and concerned at home, and pray always.

DOCTRINE AND COVENANTS 93:50

A home is much more than a house. A house is built of lumber, brick, and stone. A home is made of love, sacrifice, and respect. A house can be a home, and a home can be a heaven when it shelters a family. Like the structure in which it dwells, the family may be large or small. It may be old or young. It may be in excellent condition or it may show signs of wear, of neglect, of deterioration.

COURAGE TO WALK AWAY

There hath no temptation taken you but such as is common to man: but God is faithful, who will not suffer you to be tempted above that ye are able; but will with the temptation also make a way to escape, that ye may be able to bear it.

1 CORINTHIANS 10:13

Our Heavenly Father has counseled us to seek after "anything virtuous, lovely, or of good report or praiseworthy" (Articles of Faith 1:13). Whatever you read, listen to, or watch makes an impression on you.

Pornography is especially dangerous and addictive. Curious exploration of pornography can become a controlling habit, leading to coarser material and to sexual transgression.

Don't be afraid to walk out of a movie, turn off a television set, or change a radio station if what's being presented does not meet your Heavenly Father's standards.

IMPORTANT CRITERIA FOR YOUR LIFE'S WORK

And all this for the benefit of the church of the living God, that every man may improve upon his talent, that every man may gain other talents, yea, even an hundred fold.

DOCTRINE AND COVENANTS 82:18

Study and prepare for your life's work in a field that you enjoy, because you are going to spend a good share of your life in that field. It should be one which will challenge your intellect and which will make maximum utilization of your talents and your capabilities. Now that's a big order. But I bear testimony that these criteria are very important in choosing your life's work.

ANXIOUS TO BLESS

There should be no contention one with another,
but that they should look forward with one eye, having
one faith and one baptism, having their hearts knit
together in unity and in love one towards another.

MOSIAH 18:21

Brigham Young counseled us: "Go on until we are perfect; loving our neighbor more than we love ourselves." It is folly in the extreme for persons to say that they love god when they do not love their brethren. And the Prophet Joseph Smith advised: "A man filled with the love of God is not content with blessing his family alone, but ranges through the whole world, anxious to bless the whole human race."

This is the kind of love which fills the hearts of our missionaries who, in response to a call from God's prophet, leave the comfort of their own families and homes and go into the world to share the most precious message given to man.

MAY

*But behold, if ye will awake and arouse
your faculties, even to an experiment upon
my words, and exercise a particle of faith,
yea, even if ye can no more than desire to
believe, let this desire work in you, even
until ye believe in a manner that ye can
give place for a portion of my words.*

ALMA 32:27

SERVICE AND SUCCESS

*That ye might walk worthy of the Lord unto
all pleasing, being fruitful in every good work,
and increasing in the knowledge of God.*

COLOSSIANS 1:10

During your life you may achieve wealth or fame or social standing. Real success, however, comes from helping others. Said Ralph Waldo Emerson, noted thinker, lecturer, essayist, and poet, "To know even one life breathed easier because you have lived. This is to have succeeded."

There are opportunities to serve which are open to everyone. The blind and the handicapped need friendship; the aged are hungry for companionship; the young need understanding guidance; the gifted are starved for encouragement. These benefits can't be conferred by reaching for your checkbook. Personal service is direct and human.

ABILITY TO ENDURE

Thou therefore endure hardness,
as a good soldier of Jesus Christ.

2 TIMOTHY 2:3

We all have treasured memories of certain days in our lives—days when all seemed to go well for us, when much was accomplished or when relationships were pleasant and loving. It's not difficult to be happy on such perfect days.

Our mortal life, however, was never meant to be easy or consistently pleasant.

Our Heavenly Father, who gives us so much to delight in, also knows that we learn and grow and become refined through hard challenges, heartbreaking sorrows, and difficult choices. These and other trials present us with the real test of our ability to endure.

TO THE VERY END

I have fought a good fight,
I have finished my course,
I have kept the faith.

2 TIMOTHY 4:7

A fundamental question remains to be answered by each who runs the race of life: Shall I falter, or shall I finish? To finish life's race involves enduring through challenges and trials to the very end of life itself.

DOUBT NEVER INSPIRES FAITH

And beside this, giving all diligence,
add to your faith virtue; and to virtue knowledge.

2 PETER 1:5

The unsatisfied yearnings of the soul will not be met by a never-ending quest for joy midst the thrills of sensation and vice. Vice never leads to virtue. Hate never points to love. Cowardice never reflects courage. Doubt never inspires faith.

In the words of the poet, "Wouldst thou be gathered to Christ's chosen flock, shun the broad way too easily explored, And let thy path be hewn out of the rock, The living rock of God's eternal word" (William Wordsworth, "Inscription on a Rock at Rydal Mount").

TURNING HOMEWARD

*What therefore God hath joined together,
let not man put asunder.*

MARK 10:9

At times we may become bored or irritated with home and family and familiar surroundings. Such may seem less than glamorous, with a sense of sameness, and other places may sometimes seem more exciting. But when we have sampled much and have wandered far and have seen how fleeting and sometimes superficial a lot of the world is, our gratitude grows for the privilege of being part of something we can count on—home and family and the loyalty of loved ones. We come to know what it means to be bound together by duty, by respect, by belonging. We learn that nothing can fully take the place of the blessed relationship of family life.

LOVE IS
THE ANSWER

I know thy heart, and have heard thy prayers concerning thy brethren. Be not partial towards them in love above many others, but let thy love be for them as for thyself; and let thy love abound unto all men, and unto all who love my name.

DOCTRINE AND COVENANTS 112:11

One might ask, concerning those who assist in the welfare program, *what prompts such devotion on the part of every worker?* The answer can be stated simply: An individual testimony of the gospel of the Lord Jesus Christ, even a heartfelt desire to love the Lord with all one's heart, mind, and soul, and one's neighbor as oneself.

LEARN PATIENCE

*Thy hands have made me
and fashioned me: give me understanding,
that I may learn thy commandments.*

PSALM 119:73

I believe that I can learn patience by better studying the life of our Lord and Savior. Can you imagine the disappointment which He must have felt, knowing that He had the keys to eternal life, knowing that He had the way for you and for me to gain entrance into the celestial kingdom of God, as He took His gospel to those people in the meridian of time and saw them reject Him and reject His message? Yet He demonstrated patience. He accepted His responsibility in life, even to the cross, the Garden of Gethsemane preceding it. I would hope to learn patience from the Lord.

THE PATH TO PEACE

Therefore, renounce war and proclaim peace, and seek diligently to turn the hearts of the children to their fathers, and the hearts of the fathers to the children.

DOCTRINE AND COVENANTS 98:16

In a world where peace is such a universal quest, we sometimes wonder why violence walks our streets, accounts of murder and senseless killings fill the columns of our news papers, and family quarrels and disputes mar the sanctity of the home and smother the tranquility of so many lives.

Perhaps we stray from the path which leads to peace and find it necessary to pause, to ponder, and to reflect on the teachings of the Prince of Peace and determine to incorporate them in our thoughts and actions and to live a higher law, walk a more elevated road, and be a better disciple of Christ.

THE LORD CAN WORK THROUGH US

*I speak unto you with my voice, even the voice
of my Spirit, that I may show unto you my will
concerning your brethren in the land of Zion.*

DOCTRINE AND COVENANTS 97:1

When we let the Lord be our guide in developing communication skills, He can help us to be humble, to present ourselves to the right people at the proper time and in an atmosphere where we will be trusted and worthy of a listening ear. When communication skills are accompanied by spirituality, the Lord can work through His servants to accomplish His purposes.

A MOTHER'S LOVE

*When Jesus therefore saw his mother, and
the disciple standing by, whom he loved, he saith
unto his mother, Woman, behold thy son!*

JOHN 19:26

Who can probe a mother's love? Who can comprehend in its entirety the lofty role of a mother? With perfect trust in God, she walks, her hand in his, into the valley of the shadow of death, that you and I might come forth into light.

The holiest words my tongue can frame,
The noblest thoughts my soul can claim,
Unworthy are to praise the name
More precious than all others.
An infant, when her love first came,
A man, I find it still the same;
Reverently I breathe her name,
The blessed name of mother.

THE CAPACITY TO BE GREAT

And ye are to be taught from on high.
Sanctify yourselves and ye shall be endowed with
power, that ye may give even as I have spoken.

DOCTRINE AND COVENANTS 43:16

We know that some people are more talented than others. Some are more educated. Regardless of where we fit in the scheme of things, we all have the capacity to be great, for we are only limited by how we choose, how resolute we are—in other words, by our attitude.

NONE SHALL
BE DENIED

*They were assembled awaiting the advent
of the Son of God into the spirit world, to declare
their redemption from the bands of death.*

DOCTRINE AND COVENANTS 138:16

For those who have died without a knowledge
of the truth, a way has been provided. Sacred
ordinances can be performed by the faithful
living for the waiting dead. Houses of the Lord
known as temples dot the land. As Elijah the
prophet testified, the hearts of the fathers have
been turned to the children, and the children
to the fathers (see D&C 110:14–15). None shall
be denied. All shall have opportunity for eternal blessings.

A POWERFUL EXAMPLE

Therefore, what manner of men ought ye to be?
Verily I say unto you, even as I am.

3 NEPHI 27:27

As a boy, Jesus was found "in the temple, sitting in the midst of the doctors, both hearing them, and asking them questions. And all that heard him were astonished at his understanding and answers. And when [Joseph and His mother] saw him, they were amazed. . . . And Jesus increased in wisdom and stature, and in favour with God and man" (Luke 2:46–48, 52).

He "went about doing good, . . . for God was with him" (Acts 10:38).

I mention these powerful examples so that every man may know for himself his own strength when God is with him.

LIVE IN THE PRESENT

*Seek ye first the kingdom of God and his righteousness,
and all these things shall be added unto you.*

3 NEPHI 13:33

Daydreaming of the past and longing for the future may provide comfort but will not take the place of living in the present. This is the day of our opportunity, and we must grasp it.

Professor Harold Hill, in Meredith Willson's *The Music Man,* cautioned: "You pile up enough tomorrows, and you'll find you've collected a lot of empty yesterdays."

There is no tomorrow to remember if we don't do something today, and to live most fully today, we must do that which is of greatest importance.

WORTHY OF CELESTIAL GLORY

So God created man in his own image,
in the image of God created he him;
male and female created he them.

GENESIS 1:27

Created in the image of God. You cannot sincerely hold this conviction without experiencing a profound new sense of strength and power. As Latter-day Saints we know that we lived before we came to earth, that mortality is a probationary period where we might prove ourselves obedient to God's command and therefore worthy of celestial glory. Thus we learn who we are. Now what does God expect us to become?

"THANK YOU"

And whatsoever ye do in word or deed,
do all in the name of the Lord Jesus, giving
thanks to God and the Father by him.

COLOSSIANS 3:17

In the world of today there is at times a tendency to feel detached—even isolated—from the Giver of every good gift. We worry that we walk alone and ask, "How can we cope?" What brings ultimate comfort to us is the gospel.

Gracias, danke, merci—whatever language is spoken, "thank you," frequently expressed, will cheer your spirit, broaden your friendships, and lift your lives to a higher pathway as you journey toward perfection. There is a simplicity—even a sincerity—when "thank you" is spoken.

THE MOST IMPORTANT DUTY

Go ye therefore, and teach all nations,
baptizing them in the name of the Father,
and of the Son, and of the Holy Ghost.

MATTHEW 28:19

The holy scriptures contain no proclamation more relevant, no responsibility more binding, no instruction more direct than the injunction given by the resurrected Lord as He appeared in Galilee to the eleven disciples. The Prophet Joseph Smith declared: "After all that has been said, the greatest and most important duty is to preach the Gospel." Now is the time for members and missionaries to come together, to work together, to labor in the Lord's vineyard to bring souls unto Him. He has prepared the means for us to share the gospel in a multitude of ways, and He will assist us in our labors if we will act in faith to fulfill His work.

GUIDING
OUR FAMILIES

*They were not fighting for monarchy nor power but
they were fighting for their homes and their liberties,
their wives and their children, and their all.*

ALMA 43:45

Just a few short generations ago, one could
not have imagined the world in which we now
live and the problems it presents. We are surrounded by immorality, pornography, violence,
drugs, and a host of other ills which afflict
modern-day society. Ours is the challenge,
even the responsibility, not only to keep ourselves "unspotted from the world" (James 1:27),
but also to guide our children and others for
whom we have responsibility safely through the
stormy seas of sin surrounding all of us, that we
might one day return to live with our Heavenly
Father.

LOOK AND LIVE

Behold, he was spoken of by Moses; yea, and behold a type was raised up in the wilderness, that whosoever would look upon it might live. And many did look and live.

ALMA 33:19

Let us look heavenward. Doing so is much more inspiring. From the heavens came the gentle invitation, "Look to God and live" (Alma 37:47). We have not been left to wander in darkness and in silence uninstructed, uninspired, without revelation.

From the scriptures, from the prophets, comes counsel for our time as we look heavenward.

A PATTERN OF PREPARATION

Wherefore take unto you the whole armour
of God, that ye may be able to withstand in the
evil day, and having done all, to stand.

EPHESIANS 6:13

Preparation precedes power. To obtain the knowledge and skill we require need not be an insurmountable task if we adopt for our pattern the experience of the sons of Mosiah. Alma was journeying from the land of Gideon southward, away to the land of Manti, when he met the sons of Mosiah journeying toward the land of Zarahemla. Alma rejoiced exceedingly to see his brethren; and what added more to his joy, they were still his brethren in the Lord; yea, and they had waxed strong in the knowledge of the truth; for they were men of a sound understanding and had searched the scriptures diligently that they might know the word of God.

YOU NEVER
WALK ALONE

And whoso receiveth you, there I will be also,
for I will go before your face. I will be on your right hand
and on your left, and my Spirit shall be in your hearts,
and mine angels round about you, to bear you up.

DOCTRINE AND COVENANTS 84:88

As we seek our Heavenly Father through fervent, sincere prayer and earnest, dedicated scripture study, our testimonies will become strong and deeply rooted. We will know of God's love for us. We will understand that we do not ever walk alone. I promise you that you will one day stand aside and look at your difficult times, and you will realize that He was always there beside you. I know this to be true in the passing of my eternal companion—Frances Beverly Johnson Monson.

ANSWERING PRAYERS
THROUGH ACTION

And, inasmuch as they are faithful,
I will multiply blessings upon them and their seed
after them, even a multiplicity of blessings.

DOCTRINE AND COVENANTS 104:33

Of all the blessings which I have had in my life, the greatest blessing I can share with you is that feeling which the Lord provides when you know that He, the Lord, has answered the prayer of another person through you. As you love the Lord, as you love your neighbor, you will discover that our Heavenly Father will answer the prayers of others through your ministry.

BY DIVINE HELP

Wherefore, as ye are agents, ye are on the Lord's errand; and whatever ye do according to the will of the Lord is the Lord's business.

DOCTRINE AND COVENANTS 64:29

If we are on the Lord's errand, we are entitled to the Lord's help. That divine help, however, is predicated upon our worthiness. To sail safely the seas of mortality, to perform a human rescue mission, we need the guidance of that eternal mariner—even the great Jehovah. We reach out, we reach up, to obtain heavenly help.

A BENCHMARK
COMMANDMENT

*Behold, now it is called today until the coming
of the Son of Man, and verily it is a day of sacrifice,
and a day for the tithing of my people; for he that
is tithed shall not be burned at his coming.*

DOCTRINE AND COVENANTS 64:23

Always be active in the Church. I will give
you a formula which will guarantee to a large
extent your success in fulfilling that commitment. It is simple. It consists of just three words:
Pay your tithing. Every bishop could tell you
from his personal experience that when the
members of the Church pay tithing, honestly,
faithfully, they have little difficulty keeping the
other commandments of God. I call it a bench-
mark commandment.

THE MISSION TO SAVE SOULS

And if it so be that you should labor all your days
in crying repentance unto this people, and bring,
save it be one soul unto me, how great shall be your
joy with him in the kingdom of my Father!

DOCTRINE AND COVENANTS 18:15

Right now, today, some are caught in the current of popular opinion. Others are torn by the tide of turbulent times. Yet others are drawn down and drowned in the whirlpool of sin.

This need not be. We have the doctrines of truth. We have the programs. We have the people. We have the power. Our mission is more than meetings. Our service is to save souls.

A HAPPY CONSCIENCE

Pray for us: for we trust we have a good conscience, in all things willing to live honestly.

HEBREWS 13:18

It has been said that conscience warns us as a friend before it punishes us as a judge. The expression of one young man is a sermon in itself. When asked when he was happiest, he replied, "I'm happiest when I don't have a guilty conscience."

OUR DUTY TO OUR CHILDREN

When they came up to the temple, they pitched their tents round about, every man according to his family, consisting of his wife, and his sons, and his daughters, and their sons, and their daughters, . . . every family being separate one from another.

MOSIAH 2:5

The first and foremost opportunity for teaching in the Church lies in the home," observed President David O. McKay. "A true Mormon home is one in which if Christ should chance to enter, he would be pleased to linger and to rest" ("Gospel Ideals," *Improvement Era*, 169). What are we doing to ensure that our homes meet this description? It isn't enough for parents alone to have strong testimonies. Children can ride only so long on the coattails of a parent's conviction.

President Heber J. Grant declared: "Our children will not know that the gospel is true unless they study it and gain a testimony for themselves."

EQUAL
TO THE TASK

*For God hath not given us the spirit of fear;
but of power, and of love, and of a sound mind.*

2 TIMOTHY 1:7

All have opportunities for service to our Heavenly Father and to His children here on earth. It is contrary to the spirit of service to live selfishly within ourselves and disregard the needs of others. The Lord will guide us and make us equal to the challenges before us.

FAITH
CONQUERS FEAR

*And Alma cried, saying: How long shall we suffer these
great afflictions, O Lord? O Lord, give us strength according
to our faith which is in Christ, even unto deliverance.
And they broke the cords with which they were bound.*

ALMA 14:26

Many of the challenges we face exist because we live in this mortal world, populated by all manner of individuals. At times we ask in desperation, "How can I keep my sights firmly fixed on the celestial as I navigate through this telestial world?"

There will be times when you will walk a path strewn with thorns and marked by struggle. You worry that you walk alone. Fear replaces faith.

When you find yourself in such circumstances, I plead with you to remember prayer.

THE INFLUENCE
OF A MOTHER

*And they rehearsed unto me
the words of their mothers, saying:
We do not doubt our mothers knew it.*

ALMA 56:48

Mother," more than any other word, is held in universal esteem by all peoples everywhere. It brings forth from the soul the most tender of hidden emotions, prompts more good deeds, kindles memories' fires as they burn low, and reminds all to strive to be better. "Mother," or its abbreviated version, "Mama," is the first word tiny lips form. What joy fills mother's heart when first she hears this expression from her child. Years pass, and children become more independent. They move away from mother's protective care; but they are ever influenced by mother's teachings, mother's example, and mother's love.

ACHIEVE THE MIRACULOUS

*And faith, hope, charity and love, with an eye single
to the glory of God, qualify him for the work.*

DOCTRINE AND COVENANTS 4:5

You can make a difference. Whom the Lord calls, the Lord qualifies. When we qualify ourselves by our worthiness, when we strive with faith nothing wavering to fulfill the duties appointed to us, when we seek the inspiration of the Almighty in the performance of our responsibilities, we can achieve the miraculous.

JUNE

*Let thy bowels also be full of charity
towards all men, and to the household of
faith, and let virtue garnish thy thoughts
unceasingly; then shall thy confidence
wax strong in the presence of God.*

<small>DOCTRINE AND COVENANTS 121:45</small>

NOT ALWAYS
THE EASIEST COURSE

*And when I had said this, the Lord spake
unto me, saying: Fools mock, but they shall mourn;
and my grace is sufficient for the meek, that they
shall take no advantage of your weakness.*

ETHER 12:26

Your decision to think right, choose right, and do right will rarely if ever be the easiest course to follow. Truth has never been so popular as error. Be ready to withstand the ridicule and mockery of the uninformed, the uncultured, the uninspired. However, men and women of character stand ready to respect a man of principle, a man of courage, a man of faith.

A PERSONAL LIAHONA

*And behold, it was prepared to
show unto our fathers the course which
they should travel in the wilderness.*

ALMA 37:39

Your patriarchal blessing is yours and yours alone. It may be brief or lengthy, simple or profound. Length and language do not a patriarchal blessing make. It is the Spirit that conveys the true meaning. Your blessing is not to be folded neatly and tucked away. It is not to be framed or published. Rather, it is to be read. It is to be loved. It is to be followed. Your patriarchal blessing will see you through the darkest night. It will guide you through life's dangers. Your patriarchal blessing is to you a personal Liahona to chart your course and guide your way.

Patience may be required as we watch, wait, and work for a promised blessing to be fulfilled.

GREAT IN THE SIGHT OF GOD

*Remember the worth of souls is
great in the sight of God.*

DOCTRINE AND COVENANTS 18:10

A wise man, a noble ruler, King David, king of all Israel, once asked a question of the Lord—and this same question has been asked time and time again down through the centuries of time. He said, as recorded in the eighth Psalm, "When I consider thy heavens, the work of thy fingers, the moon and the stars, which thou hast ordained; What is man, that thou art mindful of him?" (Psalm 8:3–4).

The Lord Himself chose to give an answer to King David when He made a declaration which rings down through the years: "Remember the worth of souls is great in the sight of God" (Doctrine and Covenants 18:10).

THE HEAVENLY VIRTUE OF PATIENCE

Wherefore seeing we also are compassed about with so great a cloud of witnesses, let us lay aside every weight, and the sin which doth so easily beset us, and let us run with patience the race that is set before us.

HEBREWS 12:1

Life is full of difficulties, some minor and others of a more serious nature. There seems to be an unending supply of challenges for one and all. Our problem is that we often expect instantaneous solutions to such challenges, forgetting that frequently the heavenly virtue of patience is required.

The counsel heard in our youth is still applicable today and should be heeded. "Hold your horses," "Keep your shirt on," "Slow down," "Don't be in such a hurry," "Follow the rules," "Be careful" are more than trite expressions. They describe sincere counsel and speak the wisdom of experience.

A CHALLENGE

*I beheld that the faithful elders of this dispensation,
when they depart from mortal life, continue their labors in
the preaching of the gospel of repentance and redemption,
. . . in the great world of the spirits of the dead.*

DOCTRINE AND COVENANTS 138:57

There are thousands upon thousands, yes, millions upon millions of spirit children of our Heavenly Father who have lived here, who have never heard of the word "Christ," who have died, who have gone back to the spirit world in their state of progression and have been taught the gospel; and now they are waiting the day when you and I will do the research which is necessary to clear the way, that we might likewise go into the house of God and perform that work for them, that they, themselves, cannot perform. Are we willing to accept that challenge?

CONCERN FOR OTHERS FIRST

Let love be without dissimulation. Abhor that which is evil; cleave to that which is good. Be kindly affectioned one to another with brotherly love; in honour preferring one another.

ROMANS 12:9–10

In the helter-skelter competitiveness of life, there is a tendency to think only of ourselves. To succumb to this philosophy narrows one's vision and distorts a proper view of life. When concern for others replaces concern for self, our own progress is enhanced.

TO HUMBLY SERVE

And no one can assist in this work except he
shall be humble and full of love, having faith,
hope, and charity, being temperate in all things,
whatsoever shall be entrusted to his care.

DOCTRINE AND COVENANTS 12:8

Frustration flees, doubt disappears, and uncertainty wanes when truth is taught in boldness, yet in a spirit of humility by those who have been called to serve the Prince of Peace—even Jesus Christ.

PREPARATION PRECEDES PERFORMANCE

Now, the decrees of God are unalterable;
therefore, the way is prepared that whosoever
will may walk therein and be saved.

ALMA 41:8

Preparation for life's opportunities and responsibilities has never been more vital. We live in a changing society. Intense competition is a part of life. The role of husband, father, grandfather, provider, and protector is vastly different from what it was a generation ago. Preparation is not a matter of perhaps or maybe. It is a mandate. The old phrase "Ignorance is bliss" is forever gone. Preparation precedes performance.

LIVING WITHIN OUR MEANS

*And he said unto them, Take heed, and beware
of covetousness: for a man's life consisteth not in the
abundance of the things which he possesseth.*

LUKE 12:15

Let us be content with what we have, and make sure that we are able, if we move a little beyond, that it is not beyond our financial reach. Then we will have happier marriages. We will have fewer bankruptcies. We will have people who have that smile of being out of debt or in controlled debt, without the specter of losing their home and all they have when the inability to pay dawns upon them.

SWIMMING AGAINST THE CURRENT

Let me be weighed in an even balance,
that God may know mine integrity.

JOB 31:6

Being true to oneself is anything but easy if the moral standards of one's associates conflict with his or her own. The herd instinct is strong in the human animal, and the phrase "Everybody else is doing it" has an insidious attraction. To resist what "everybody else" is doing is to risk being ostracized by one's peers, and it's normal to dread rejection. Nothing takes more strength than swimming against the current.

STAND ABOVE THE WAYS OF THE WORLD

I have given them thy word; and the world hath hated them, because they are not of the world, even as I am not of the world.

JOHN 17:14

The Savior of mankind described Himself as being in the world but not of the world. We also can be in the world but not of the world as we reject false concepts and false teachings and remain true to that which God has commanded.

President Hinckley taught that it is up to each of us to discipline ourselves so that we stand above the ways of the world. It is essential that we be honorable and decent. Our actions must be above reproach.

The words we speak, the way we treat others, and the way we live our lives all impact our effectiveness.

THE DOOR TO LEARNING

A wise man will hear, and will increase learning;
and a man of understanding shall attain unto wise counsels.

PROVERBS 1:5

Education is a process, not a completed act. The prescriptions of our times look as though you'll go through the motions of an education whether you want to or not. You don't need to ask anymore for an educational opportunity. You have only to knock to take advantage of it. But to achieve excellence, you must open the door to learning yourself. Contrary to what we'd like to believe, excellence in education is rarely unearned. In our quest for knowledge, there is no room for cheating, for dishonesty, for that which would degrade us or cause the loss of our precious self-respect.

FIND JOY NOW

Now was not this exceeding joy? Behold,
this is joy which none receiveth save it be the truly
penitent and humble seeker of happiness.

ALMA 27:18

Each one of you is living a life filled with much to do. I plead with you not to let the important things in life pass you by, planning instead for that illusive and nonexistent future day when you'll have time to do all that you want to do. Instead, find joy in the journey—now.

"LET IT BEGIN WITH ME"

But ye, brethren, be not weary in well doing.

2 THESSALONIANS 3:13

In this world in which we live, there is a tendency for us to describe needed change, required help, and desired relief with the familiar phrase, "They ought to do something about this." We fail to define the word *they*. I love the message, "Let there be peace on earth, and let it begin with me."

I extol those who, with loving care and compassionate concern, feed the hungry, clothe the naked, and house the homeless. He who notes the sparrow's fall will not be unmindful of such service.

THAT WHICH WE DESIRE MOST

The natural man receiveth not the things of the Spirit of God: for they are foolishness unto him: neither can he know them, because they are spiritually discerned.

1 CORINTHIANS 2:14

It may appear to you at times that those out in the world are having much more fun than you are. Some of you may feel restricted by the code of conduct to which we in the Church adhere. My brothers and sisters, I declare to you, however, that there is nothing which can bring more joy into our lives or more peace to our souls than the Spirit which can come to us as we follow the Savior and keep the commandments. We must be vigilant in a world which has moved so far from the spiritual. It is essential that we reject anything that does not conform to our standards, refusing to surrender that which we desire most: eternal life in the kingdom of God.

THE CHOICE IS OURS

That every man may act in doctrine and principle pertaining to futurity, according to the moral agency which I have given unto him, that every man may be accountable for his own sins in the day of judgment.

DOCTRINE AND COVENANTS 101:78

You are provided the God-given blessing of free agency. The pathway is marked. The blessings and penalties are shown clearly. But the choice is up to you. Of course there will be opposition. There always has been and always will be. That evil one, even Satan, desires that you become his follower, rather than a leader in your own right. He has evil and designing men as his agents. In a most enticing manner he cunningly invites: "This is the way to happiness; come." Yet that still, small voice within you cautions: "Not so. This doesn't seem right." A choice has to be made. There are no minor or insignificant decisions in your life.

THIS GREAT CAUSE

And at all times, and in all places, he shall open his mouth and declare my gospel as with the voice of a trump, both day and night. And I will give unto him strength such as is not known among men.

DOCTRINE AND COVENANTS 24:12

This great cause in which we are engaged will continue to go forth, changing and blessing lives as it does so. No cause, no force in the entire world can stop the work of God. Despite what comes, this great cause will go forward. You recall the prophetic words of the Prophet Joseph Smith: "No unhallowed hand can stop the work from progressing; persecutions may rage, mobs may combine, armies may assemble, calumny may defame, but the truth of God will go forth boldly, nobly, and independent, till . . . the Great Jehovah shall say the work is done" (*Teachings of Presidents of the Church: Joseph Smith*, 444).

PRIVILEGED TO CHOOSE

Thou hast commanded us to keep thy precepts diligently.
O that my ways were directed to keep thy statutes!

PSALM 119:4–5

How grateful we should be that a wise Creator fashioned an earth and placed us here, with a veil of forgetfulness of our previous existence, so that we might experience a time of testing, an opportunity to prove ourselves, and qualify for all that God has prepared for us to receive. Clearly, one primary purpose of our existence upon the earth is to obtain a body of flesh and bones. In a thousand ways, we are privileged to choose for ourselves. Here we learn from the hard taskmaster of experience. We discern between good and evil. We differentiate as to the bitter and the sweet. We discover that decisions determine destiny.

THE PATHWAY
TO DIVINE TRUTH

*If my people, which are called by my name, shall
humble themselves, and pray, and seek my face, and turn
from their wicked ways; then will I hear from heaven,
and will forgive their sin, and will heal their land.*

2 CHRONICLES 7:14

By seeking God in personal and family
prayer, we and our loved ones will develop the
fulfillment of what the great English statesman
William H. Gladstone described as the world's
greatest need: "A living faith in a personal
God." Who can evaluate the real worth of such
a blessing? Such a faith will light the pathway
for any honest seeker of divine truth.

FACING UNCERTAINTIES

For God doth not walk in crooked paths, neither doth he turn to the right hand nor to the left, neither doth he vary from that which he hath said, therefore his paths are straight, and his course is one eternal round.

DOCTRINE AND COVENANTS 3:2

As we pursue our quest for eternal life, we will come to many forks and turnings in the road. We cannot venture into the uncertainties of the future without reference to the certainties of the past. Your challenge is to join the forces of the old and the new—experience and experiment, history and destiny, the world of man and the world of science—but always in accordance with the never-changing word of God. In short, He becomes your pilot on this eternal journey. He knows the way. His counsel can keep us from the pitfalls threatening to engulf us and lead us rather to the way of life eternal.

A ROYAL ARMY

Behold, I will send for many fishers, saith the Lord,
and they shall fish them; and after will I send for many
hunters, and they shall hunt them from every mountain,
and from every hill, and out of the holes of the rocks.

JEREMIAH 16:16

The priesthood represents a mighty army of righteousness—even a royal army. We are led by a prophet of God. In supreme command is our Lord and Savior, Jesus Christ. Our marching orders are clear. They are concise. Matthew describes our challenge in these words from the Master: "Go ye therefore, and teach all nations, baptizing them in the name of the Father, and of the Son, and of the Holy Ghost" (Matthew 28:19).

BACK TO BASICS

And I, the Lord God, said unto mine Only Begotten,
that it was not good that the man should be alone;
wherefore, I will make an help meet for him.

MOSES 3:18

When the seas of life are stormy, a wise mariner seeks a port of peace. The family, as we have traditionally known it, is such a refuge of safety. The tremendous increase in the number of single parents has been one of the most profound changes in family composition to have occurred during the past quarter century. All of us are acutely aware of the devastation of divorce and other negative influences in our society that stalk the traditional family.

What is the solution? Where is our answer to be found? "Back to Basics" may well be a formula to give us help. The home is the basis of a righteous life.

PROTECTION IN TROUBLED TIMES

Watch and pray always lest ye enter into temptation; for Satan desireth to have you, that he may sift you as wheat. Therefore ye must always pray unto the Father in my name.

3 Nephi 18:18–19

We have come to the earth in troubled times. The moral compass of the masses has gradually shifted to an "almost anything goes" position.

I've lived long enough to have witnessed much of the metamorphosis of society's morals. Where once the standards of the Church and the standards of society were mostly compatible, now there is a wide chasm between us, and it's growing ever wider.

What will protect you from the sin and evil around you? I maintain that a strong testimony of our Savior and of His gospel will help see you through to safety.

THE SINGLE MOST IMPORTANT WORD

The Lord hath appeared of old unto me, saying,
Yea, I have loved thee with an everlasting love:
therefore with lovingkindness have I drawn thee.

JEREMIAH 31:3

Robert Woodruff, an executive in a former generation, traversed America with a message which he delivered to civic and business groups. The outline was simple, the message brief:

The five most important words are these:
I am proud of you.

The four most important words are these:
What is your opinion?

The three most important words are these:
If you please.

The two most important words are these:
Thank you.

To Mr. Woodruff's list I would add, "The single most important word is *love*."

PRICELESS COMFORT

As one whom his mother comforteth,
so will I comfort you.

ISAIAH 66:13

In the world of today there is at times a tendency to feel detached—even isolated—from the Giver of every good gift. We worry that we walk alone and ask, "How can we cope?" What brings ultimate comfort to us is the gospel. From the bed of pain, from the pillow wet with tears, we are lifted heavenward by that divine assurance and precious promise: "I will not fail thee, nor forsake thee" (Joshua 1:5). Such comfort is priceless as we journey along the pathway of mortality. Rarely is the assurance communicated by a flashing sign or a loud voice. Rather, the language of the Spirit is gentle, quiet, uplifting to the heart, and soothing to the soul.

TEACH THE WAY TO PERFECTION

I, the Lord, am merciful and gracious unto those who fear me, and delight to honor those who serve me in righteousness and in truth unto the end.

DOCTRINE AND COVENANTS 76:5

The calling of the early Apostles reflected the influence of the Lord. When He sought a man of faith, He did not select him from the throng of the self-righteous who were found regularly in the synagogue. Rather, He called him from among the fishermen of Capernaum. Simon, man of doubt, became Peter, Apostle of faith. Saul of Tarsus—the persecutor—became Paul the proselyter.

The Redeemer chose imperfect men to teach the way to perfection. He did so then; He does so now. He calls you and me to serve Him here below and sets us to the task He would have us fulfill.

FOR THOSE WHO WAIT BEYOND THE VEIL

The dead who repent will be redeemed, through obedience to the ordinances of the house of God.

DOCTRINE AND COVENANTS 138:58

Today most of us do not have to suffer great hardships in order to attend the temple. Eighty-five percent of the membership of the Church now lives within 200 miles (320 km) of a temple, and for a great many of us, that distance is much shorter. If you have been to the temple for yourselves and if you live within relatively close proximity to a temple, your sacrifice could be setting aside the time in your busy lives to visit the temple regularly. There is much to be done in our temples in behalf of those who wait beyond the veil. As we do the work for them, we will know that we have accomplished what they cannot do for themselves.

THE LIVING GOD

*The Father has a body of flesh and bones as tangible
as man's; the Son also; but the Holy Ghost has not
a body of flesh and bones, but is a personage of Spirit.
Were it not so, the Holy Ghost could not dwell in us.*

DOCTRINE AND COVENANTS 130:22

God our Father has ears with which to hear
our prayers. He has eyes with which to see our
actions. He has a mouth with which to speak to
us. He has a heart with which to feel compassion and love. He is real. He is living.

A RECIPE FOR GETTING THINGS DONE

Do not procrastinate the day of your repentance
until the end; . . . behold, if we do not improve
our time while in this life, then cometh the night
of darkness wherein there can be no labor performed.

ALMA 34:33

Two twins stand before us, about whom we must make a choice. They are: "Do it now" and "Put it off." Remember, decision is of little account unless it is followed by action, and there is no recipe for getting things done so good as the one to start doing them.

FROM FAILURE TO ACHIEVEMENT

*And behold, he that is faithful shall
be made ruler over many things.*

DOCTRINE AND COVENANTS 52:13

In our journey on earth, we discover that life is made up of challenges—they just differ from one person to another. We are success-oriented, striving to become "wonder women" and "super men." Any intimation of failure can cause panic, even despair. Who among us cannot remember moments of failure?

Our responsibility is to rise from mediocrity to competence, from failure to achievement. Our task is to become our best selves. One of God's greatest gifts to us is the joy of trying again, for no failure ever need be final.

JULY

The Lord is my light and my salvation;
whom shall I fear? the Lord is the strength
of my life; of whom shall I be afraid?

PSALM 27:1

TOUCHING HEAVEN

He who receiveth all things with
thankfulness shall be made glorious.

DOCTRINE AND COVENANTS 78:19

To express gratitude is gracious and honorable, to enact gratitude is generous and noble, but to live with gratitude ever in our hearts is to touch heaven.

BLUEPRINTS FOR ETERNITY

Organize yourselves; prepare every needful thing;
and establish a house, even a house of prayer, a
house of fasting, a house of faith, a house of learning,
a house of glory, a house of order, a house of God.

DOCTRINE AND COVENANTS 88:119

In a revelation given through the Prophet Joseph Smith at Kirtland, Ohio, December 27, 1832, the Master counseled: "Organize yourselves; prepare every needful thing; and establish a house, even a house of prayer, a house of fasting, a house of faith, a house of learning, a house of glory, a house of order, a house of God" (Doctrine and Covenants 88:119).

Where could any of us locate a more suitable blueprint whereby we could wisely and properly build a house to personally occupy throughout eternity?

HONORING OUR SACRED MISSION

Though he were a Son, yet learned he obedience by the things which he suffered; And being made perfect, he became the author of eternal salvation unto all them that obey him.

HEBREWS 5:8–9

The Savior demonstrated genuine love of God by living the perfect life, by honoring the sacred mission that was His. Never was He haughty. Never was He puffed up with pride. Never was He disloyal. Ever was He humble. Ever was He sincere. Ever was He obedient.

Though He was tempted by that master of deceit, even the devil, though He was physically weakened from fasting 40 days and 40 nights and was an hungered, yet when the evil one proffered Jesus the most alluring and tempting proposals, He gave to us a divine example of obedience by refusing to deviate from what He knew was right.

LEADERS IN RIGHTEOUSNESS

And inasmuch as ye shall keep my commandments,
ye shall prosper, and shall be led to a land of promise;
yea, even a land which I have prepared for you; yea,
a land which is choice above all other lands.

1 NEPHI 2:20

One of the most famous enlistment posters of World War II was one depicting Uncle Sam pointing his long finger and directing his piercing eyes at the viewer. The words read, "America Needs You." America truly does need you and me to lead out in a mighty crusade of righteousness. We can help when we love God and with our families serve Him; and when we love our neighbor as ourselves.

THE PLEASURE
OF GOOD BOOKS

*And as all have not faith, seek ye diligently
and teach one another words of wisdom; yea, seek
ye out of the best books words of wisdom;
seek learning, even by study and also by faith.*

DOCTRINE AND COVENANTS 88:118

Reading is one of the true pleasures of life. In our age of mass culture, when so much that we encounter is abridged, adapted, adulterated, shredded, and boiled down, and commercialism's loudspeakers are incessantly braying, it is mind-easing and mind-inspiring to sit down privately with a good book. It is ennobling when that book contains the revealed word of God.

SPECTATORS OR PARTICIPANTS?

And ye cannot bear all things now; nevertheless,
be of good cheer, for I will lead you along.
The kingdom is yours and the blessings thereof are
yours, and the riches of eternity are yours.

DOCTRINE AND COVENANTS 78:18

The world is in need of your help. There are feet to steady, hands to grasp, minds to encourage, hearts to inspire, and souls to save. The blessings of eternity await you. Yours is the privilege to be not spectators but participants on the stage of priesthood service.

TWO BY TWO

Behold, I am a disciple of Jesus Christ, the Son of God.
I have been called of him to declare his word among
his people, that they might have everlasting life.

3 NEPHI 5:13

All of us united as one can qualify for the guiding influence of our Heavenly Father as we pursue our respective callings. We are engaged in the work of the Lord Jesus Christ. We, like those of olden times, have answered His call. We are on His errand. We shall succeed in the solemn charge given by Mormon to declare the Lord's word among His people.

MAKE THE WORLD A LITTLE BETTER

Make you perfect in every good work to do his will, working in you that which is wellpleasing in his sight, through Jesus Christ; to whom be glory for ever and ever. Amen.

HEBREWS 13:21

One hundred years from now it will not matter what kind of a car you drove, what kind of a house you lived in, how much you had in the bank, nor what your clothes looked like. But the world may be a little better because you were important in the life of a boy or a girl.

PRAYERS HEARD AND ANSWERED

Be thou humble; and the Lord thy God shall lead thee by the hand, and give thee answer to thy prayers.

DOCTRINE AND COVENANTS 112:10

Reinforced constantly during my own review of the years has been my knowledge that our prayers are heard and answered. We are familiar with the truth found in 2 Nephi in the Book of Mormon: "Men are, that they might have joy" (2 Nephi 2:25). I testify that much of that joy comes as we recognize that we can communicate with our Heavenly Father through prayer and that those prayers will be heard and answered—perhaps not how and when we expected they would be answered, but they will be answered, and by a Heavenly Father who knows and loves us perfectly and who desires our happiness.

REMEMBER THOSE WHO HAVE GONE BEFORE

Do ye not remember that our father, Lehi, was brought out of Jerusalem by the hand of God? Do ye not remember that they were all led by him through the wilderness?

ALMA 9:9

Should you become discouraged or feel burdened down, remember that others have passed this same way; they have endured and then have achieved. When we have done all that we are able to do, we can then rely on God's promised help.

THE ULTIMATE REPORT CARD

These are they whose bodies are celestial, whose glory is that of the sun, even the glory of God, the highest of all, whose glory the sun of the firmament is written of as being typical.

DOCTRINE AND COVENANTS 76:70

It is the celestial glory which we seek. It is in the presence of God we desire to dwell. It is a forever family in which we want membership. Such blessings are earned. A high report card of mortality qualifies us to graduate with honors.

LIVING WITHIN OUR MEANS

The wicked borroweth, and payeth not again:
but the righteous sheweth mercy, and giveth.

PSALM 37:21

Many of our young couples today want to begin with multiple cars and the type of home Mother and Dad worked a lifetime to obtain. Consequently, they enter into long-term debt on the basis of two salaries. Perhaps too late they find that changes do come, women have children, sickness stalks some families, jobs are lost, natural disasters and other situations occur, and no longer can the mortgage payment, based on the income from two salaries, be made.

It is essential for us to live within our means.

FAMILY HOME EVENING

*But I have commanded you to bring up
your children in light and truth.*

DOCTRINE AND COVENANTS 93:40

We can and should emphasize family home evening. With the world seemingly growing more and more coarse, and with corrupting influences more widespread and common, the stability of homes and families is under increasing attack. Fathers and mothers are missing golden opportunities to fortify their families against the destructive influences of the day when they do not bring their families together consistently and regularly to build family unity and individual maturity and responsibilities.

LOVE THAT NEVER CHANGES

*A new commandment I give unto you,
That ye love one another; as I have loved
you, that ye also love one another.*

JOHN 13:34

Your Heavenly Father loves you—each of you. That love never changes. It is not influenced by your appearance, by your possessions, or by the amount of money you have in your bank account. It is not changed by your talents and abilities. It is simply there. It is there for you when you are sad or happy, discouraged or hopeful. God's love is there for you whether or not you feel you deserve love. It is simply always there.

CHOICES THAT BRING JOY

Now therefore, if ye will obey my voice indeed, and keep my covenant, then ye shall be a peculiar treasure unto me above all people: for all the earth is mine.

EXODUS 19:5

If we choose to do that which is right, if we will be responsible in our choices, then the results of our choices will bring joy and happiness to our souls, for the Lord has told us, "I, the Lord, am merciful and gracious unto those who fear me, and delight to honor those who serve me in righteousness and in truth unto the end" (Doctrine and Covenants 76:5).

I pray that our choice today will be that of serving the Lord in truth and in righteousness unto the end, that our Savior, our Mediator, our Lord Jesus Christ, of whom I testify, will be by our side and direct us throughout our lives and into eternity.

THE BATTLE FOR SELF-MASTERY

I give unto men weakness that they may be humble; and my grace is sufficient for all men that humble themselves before me; for if they humble themselves before me, and have faith in me, then will I make weak things become strong unto them.

ETHER 12:27

One of the imperative requirements of life is to be able to make choices. In order to do so one must know how to look at things and oneself. One must also learn that to live means being able to cope with difficulties; problems are a normal part of life, and the great thing is to avoid being flattened by them.

The battle for self-mastery may leave you a bit bruised and battered, but always a better man or woman.

Endure and Overcome

Behold, we count them happy which endure. Ye have heard of the patience of Job, and have seen the end of the Lord; that the Lord is very pitiful, and of tender mercy.

James 5:11

It may safely be assumed that no person has ever lived entirely free of suffering and tribulation, nor has there ever been a period in human history that did not have its full share of turmoil, ruin, and misery. When the pathway of life takes a cruel turn, there is the temptation to ask the question, "Why me?" Self-incrimination is a common practice, even when we may have had no control over our difficulty. Whenever we are inclined to feel burdened down with the blows of life, let us remember that others have passed the same way, have endured, and then have overcome.

TO ENSURE
A SAFE RETURN

The race is not to the swift,
nor the battle to the strong.

ECCLESIASTES 9:11

We have been provided divine attributes to guide our journey. We enter mortality not to float with the moving currents of life, but with the power to think, to reason, and to achieve.

Our Heavenly Father did not launch us on our eternal voyage without providing the means whereby we could receive from Him guidance to ensure our safe return. Yes, I speak of prayer. I speak, too, of the whisperings from that still, small voice within each of us; and I do not overlook the holy scriptures, written by mariners who successfully sailed the seas we too must cross.

COMMITTED TO OUR GOALS

Verily I say, men should be engaged in a good cause, and do many things of their own free will, and bring to pass much righteousness.

DOCTRINE AND COVENANTS 58:27

There are countless worthy goals to reach as we travel through life. Needed is our commitment to reach them.

HOLY WORDS OF TRUTH AND LOVE

And it came to pass that there came a voice unto them, yea, a pleasant voice, as if it were a whisper, saying: Peace be unto you, because of your faith in my Well Beloved, who was from the foundation of the world.

HELAMAN 5:46–47

Allied with prayer in helping us cope in our often difficult world is scripture study. The words of truth and inspiration found in our four standard works are prized possessions to me. I never tire of reading them. I am lifted spiritually whenever I search the scriptures. These holy words of truth and love give guidance to my life and point the way to eternal perfection.

As we read and ponder the scriptures, we will experience the sweet whisperings of the Spirit to our souls. When scripture study is combined with our prayers, we can of a certainty know that the gospel of Jesus Christ is true.

THE MASTER HIGHWAY BUILDER

Behold, God is my salvation; I will trust,
and not be afraid: for the Lord Jehovah is my strength
and my song; he also is become my salvation.

ISAIAH 12:2

The way to exaltation is not a freeway featuring unlimited vision, unrestricted speeds, and untested skills. Rather, it is known by many forks and turnings, sharp curves, and controlled speeds. Your driving skill will be put to the test. Are you ready? You're driving. You haven't passed this way before. Fortunately, the Master Highway Builder, even our Heavenly Father, has provided a road map showing the route to follow. He has placed markers along the way to guide you to your destination.

THE CROWNING BLESSING

*That my covenant people may be gathered
in one in that day when I shall come to my temple.
And this I do for the salvation of my people.*

DOCTRINE AND COVENANTS 42:36

If you have not yet been to the temple or if you have been but currently do not qualify for a recommend, there is no more important goal for you to work toward than being worthy to go to the temple.

Until you have entered the house of the Lord and have received all the blessings which await you there, you have not obtained everything the Church has to offer. The all-important and crowning blessings of membership in the Church are those blessings which we receive in the temples of God.

NO DECISION IS
TOO SMALL

For thus saith the scripture:
Choose ye this day, whom ye will serve.

ALMA 30:8

No decision that Latter-day Saints must make is minor or unimportant, for every decision has a bearing upon our eternal welfare. I would urge you to stay close to the Lord. Call upon Him for guidance and for help in the choices which are placed before you. The results of these choices can be good, or they can be very damaging. They can have a bearing upon another's spiritual welfare through eternity, as well as directing one's own spiritual attainment.

PIONEER COURAGE

*Be of good courage, and let us behave ourselves
valiantly for our people, and for the cities of our God:
and let the Lord do that which is good in his sight.*

1 CHRONICLES 19:13

I wonder how we would have felt if we lived in
Nauvoo with our beautiful brick home with all
of the comforts of life—and then heard the call
to move westward, to leave our homes, to leave
our families in some cases, to leave behind the
beautiful greenery and put our vision westward
to the valleys of the great Salt Lake, where one
tree greeted us upon our arrival as pioneers.
Yet, where would we have been today were it
not for the courage of the Latter-day Saints to
expand the frontiers of the Church?

YOU CAN'T BUY TIME

For there are more treasures
than one for you in this city.

DOCTRINE AND COVENANTS 111:10

So frequently we mistakenly believe that our children need more things, when in reality their silent pleadings are simply for more of our time. The accumulation of wealth or the multiplication of assets belies the Master's teachings:

"Lay not up for yourselves treasures upon earth, where moth and rust doth corrupt, and where thieves break through and steal:

"But lay up for yourselves treasures in heaven, where neither moth nor rust doth corrupt, and where thieves do not break through nor steal:

"For where your treasure is, there will your heart be also" (Matthew 6:19–21).

GOD'S LAWS ARE CONSTANT

*Moreover I will establish his kingdom
for ever, if he be constant to do my commandments
and my judgments, as at this day.*

1 CHRONICLES 28:7

Although the world has changed, the laws of God remain constant. They have not changed; they will not change. The Ten Commandments are just that—commandments. They are not suggestions. They are every bit as requisite today as they were when God gave them to the children of Israel. If we but listen, we hear the echo of God's voice, speaking to us here and now. Our code of conduct is definitive; it is not negotiable. It is found not only in the Ten Commandments but also in the Sermon on the Mount, given to us by the Savior when He walked upon the earth. It is found throughout His teachings. It is found in the words of modern revelation.

CONSIDER THE BLESSINGS

Sing unto the Lord, O ye saints of his,
and give thanks at the remembrance of his holiness.

PSALM 30:4

We are blessed with so very much. And yet it is sometimes difficult to view the problems and permissiveness around us and not become discouraged. I have found that, rather than dwelling on the negative, if we will take a step back and consider the blessings in our lives, including seemingly small, sometimes overlooked blessings, we can find greater happiness.

HALLMARKS OF A HAPPY HOME

*And it came to pass that we
lived after the manner of happiness.*

2 Nephi 5:27

Happy homes come in a variety of appearances. Some feature large families with father, mother, brothers, and sisters living together in a spirit of love. Others consist of a single parent with one or two children, while other homes have but one occupant. There are, however, identifying features which are to be found in a happy home, whatever the number or description of its family members. I refer to these as "Hallmarks of a Happy Home." They consist of:

1. A pattern of prayer.
2. A library of learning.
3. A legacy of love.
4. A treasury of testimony.

BECOMING TRUE SHEPHERDS

I am the good shepherd:
the good shepherd giveth his life for the sheep.

JOHN 10:11

There is one Teacher whose life overshadows all others. He taught of life and death, of duty and destiny. He lived not to be served but to serve, not to receive but to give, not to save His life but to sacrifice it for others.

I speak of the Master Teacher, even Jesus Christ, the Son of God, the Savior and Redeemer of all mankind. The biblical account says of Him, He "went about doing good" (Acts 10:38). With Him as our unfailing guide and exemplar, we shall qualify for His divine help. Lives will be blessed. Hearts will be comforted. Souls will be saved. We will become true shepherds.

HIS HANDS

That they may see, and know, and consider, and understand together, that the hand of the Lord hath done this, and the Holy One of Israel hath created it.

ISAIAH 41:20

The Lord declared: "Fear thou not; for I am with thee: be not dismayed; for I am thy God: . . . I will uphold thee with the right hand of my righteousness" (Isaiah 41:10). This was the determined hand which drove from the temple the money changers. This was the loving hand that opened deaf ears and restored vision to sightless eyes. By this hand was the leper cleansed, the lame man healed—even the dead Lazarus raised to life. With the finger of his hand there was written in the sand that message which the winds did erase but which honest hearts did retain. The hand of the carpenter. The hand of the teacher. The hand of Christ.

OUR RESPONSIBILITY TO TEACH

*And they shall also teach their children to pray,
and to walk uprightly before the Lord.*

DOCTRINE AND COVENANTS 68:28

To an alarming extent, our children today are being educated by the media, including the Internet. The messages portrayed on television, in movies, and in other media are very often in direct opposition to that which we want our children to embrace and hold dear. It is our responsibility not only to teach them to be sound in spirit and doctrine but also to help them stay that way, regardless of the outside forces they may encounter. This will require much time and effort on our part—and in order to help others, we ourselves need the spiritual and moral courage to withstand the evil we see on every side.

AUGUST

And the Lord called his people Zion,
because they were of one heart and
one mind, and dwelt in righteousness;
and there was no poor among them.

MOSES 7:18

HASTENING THE WORK

Behold, I will
hasten my work in its time.

DOCTRINE AND COVENANTS 88:73

His work embraces eternity, and if He indicated, as He did in the 88th section of the Doctrine and Covenants, that He would hasten His work in His time, I am simple enough to believe in my faith that our Heavenly Father is hastening His work in the spirit world and that He is bringing many souls into a period of preparation and readiness, that we might go into the temple of God and perform the sacred ordinances which will bring to those spirit children who have gone beyond, having lived in mortality, the same opportunities that you and I have. I firmly believe that He is hastening His work.

DARE TO
STAND ALONE

For I know that God is not a partial God,
neither a changeable being; but he is unchangeable
from all eternity to all eternity.

MORONI 8:18

As we go about living from day to day, it is almost inevitable that our faith will be challenged. We may at times find ourselves surrounded by others and yet standing in the minority or even standing alone concerning what is acceptable and what is not. Do we have the moral courage to stand firm for our beliefs, even if by so doing we must stand alone? It is essential that we are able to face—with courage—whatever challenges come our way. Remember the words of Tennyson: "My strength is as the strength of ten, because my heart is pure" ("Sir Galahad," in *Poems of the English Race*, 296).

HUMBLE SERVICE

But I say unto you, Love your enemies,
bless them that curse you, do good to them that hate
you, and pray for them which despitefully
use you, and persecute you.

MATTHEW 5:44

So often the call to serve is not accompanied by the sound of a marching band, the cheering crowd, or the applause of those whose favor is deemed so great. Such distractions were not to be found on Damascus way, in Palmyra's grove, on Moriah's mount, in Gethsemane's garden, nor atop Golgotha's hill.

Training Our Families

Train up a child in the way he should go:
and when he is old, he will not depart from it.

PROVERBS 22:6

The training of our own families requires our presence, our time, our best efforts. To be effective in our training, we must be stalwart in our examples to our family members and available for private time with each member, as well as time for counseling and guidance.

SPIRITUAL BUILDING BLOCKS

And all saints who remember to keep and do these sayings, walking in obedience to the commandments, shall receive health in their navel and marrow to their bones; And shall find wisdom and great treasures of knowledge, even hidden treasures.

DOCTRINE AND COVENANTS 89:18–19

Tabernacles and temples are built with more than stone and mortar, wood and glass. Particularly is this true when we speak of the temple described by the Apostle Paul: "Know ye not that ye are the temple of God, and that the Spirit of God dwelleth in you?" (1 Corinthians 3:16). Such temples are built with faith and fasting. They are built with service and sacrifice. They are built with trials and testimonies.

BELIEVE

Be not afraid, only believe.

MARK 5:36

I mention a signal which is basic and essential: *believe*. Believe that you are a son or daughter of Heavenly Father, that He loves you, and that you are here for a glorious purpose—to gain your eternal salvation. Believe that remaining strong and faithful to the truths of the gospel is of utmost importance. I testify that it is!

BEING PREPARED

*Be thou prepared, and prepare for thyself, thou,
and all thy company that are assembled unto
thee, and be thou a guard unto them.*

EZEKIEL 38:7

Scouting's motto, "Be Prepared," has universal application. Being prepared does not mean learning a set of hard and fast rules. It includes being prepared to live in a world of change, to live with uncertainty and yet to act with confidence. We must be prepared to modify yesterday's understandings in the light of today's knowledge so that we can move confidently into tomorrow's world.

LOVE SHOWN
DAY BY DAY

He that hath my commandments,
and keepeth them, he it is that loveth me: and he
that loveth me shall be loved of my Father, and I
will love him, and will manifest myself to him.

JOHN 14:21

The oft-repeated statement is yet ever true: Actions speak louder than words. And the actions whereby we demonstrate that we truly do love God and our neighbor as ourselves will rarely be such as to attract the gaze and admiration of the world. Usually our love will be shown in our day-by-day associations with one another.

WHAT TYPE OF HOME WILL WE BUILD?

*For this cause shall a man leave
his father and mother, and cleave to his wife.*

MARK 10:7

All of us remember the home of our childhood. Interestingly, our thoughts do not dwell on whether the house was large or small, the neighborhood fashionable or downtrodden. Rather, we delight in the experiences we shared as a family. The home is the laboratory of our lives, and what we learn there largely determines what we do when we leave there.

We are responsible for the home we build. We must build wisely, for eternity is not a short voyage. There will be calm and wind, sunlight and shadows, joy and sorrow. But if we really try, our home can be a bit of heaven here on earth.

SCHOOLING AND EDUCATION

And if a person gains more knowledge and intelligence in this life through his diligence and obedience than another, he will have so much the advantage in the world to come.

DOCTRINE AND COVENANTS 130:19

Someone has said that learning is not just an in-class activity, but an all-day, everywhere process. It is not all formal, rarely neat, and not at all cut-and-made-to-order. Maybe that is why it is so challenging. Schooling and education are not the same thing. Education is a process to which one is subjected throughout life. Schooling is only part of that process, covering but a fraction of a normal life span.

STOP, LOOK, AND LISTEN

*For as the heavens are higher than the
earth, so are my ways higher than your ways,
and my thoughts than your thoughts.*

ISAIAH 55:9

Today in our hurried and hectic lives, we could well go back to an earlier time for the lesson taught us regarding crossing dangerous streets. "Stop, look, and listen" were the watchwords. Could we not apply them now? Stop from a reckless road to ruin. Look upward for heavenly help. Listen for His invitation: "Come unto me, all ye that labour and are heavy laden, and I will give you rest" (Matthew 11:28).

CHANGE THE LABEL

Ye also outwardly appear righteous unto men,
but within ye are full of hypocrisy and iniquity.

MATTHEW 23:28

The Master declared to one group: "Woe unto you, scribes and Pharisees, hypocrites! for ye are like unto whited sepulchres, which indeed appear beautiful outward, but are within full of dead men's bones, and of all uncleanness" (Matthew 23:27).

Then there are those who may outwardly appear impoverished, without talent, and doomed to mediocrity. A classic label appeared beneath a picture of the boy Abraham Lincoln. The words read: "Ill-housed, ill-clothed, ill-fed." Unanticipated, unspoken, and unprinted was the real label of the boy: "Destined for immortal glory."

A Vital Work

*And he shall turn the heart of the fathers to the
children, and the heart of the children to their fathers,
lest I come and smite the earth with a curse.*

MALACHI 4:6

In our efforts to save the living, we must not
neglect those who lived and died without the
blessings provided by the temples of God. Our
renewed efforts are urgently required. This vital work cannot be postponed or neglected.

As we organize our personal and family gene-
alogical efforts, we will be in a position to take
full advantage of the computer techniques now
available and soon to be expanded and per-
fected for our benefit and the advancement of
the work of the Lord. We pray for temples, but
temples cannot function without the genealog-
ical work which is essential to their operation.

GO AND DO

*Be ye doers of the word,
and not hearers only.*

JAMES 1:22

If I were to ask you which of all the passages in the Book of Mormon is the most widely read, I venture it would be the account concerning the command to obtain the plates of brass. Said Nephi, "I will go and do the things which the Lord hath commanded, for I know that the Lord giveth no commandments unto the children of men, save he shall prepare a way for them that they may accomplish the thing which he commandeth them" (1 Nephi 3:7).

Whatever our calling, regardless of our fears or anxieties, let us pray and then go and do.

ON THE LORD'S SIDE

*Then Moses stood in the gate of the camp, and said,
Who is on the Lord's side? let him come unto me. And all
the sons of Levi gathered themselves together unto him.*

EXODUS 32:26

We are the product of all we read, all we view, all we hear and all we think. I join you in a united determination to so think, to so read, and to so hear—and I might also add to so feel—that we may evidence that we are on the Lord's side.

THE THIEF OF OUR SELF-RESPECT

Remember that without faith you can do nothing;
therefore ask in faith. Trifle not with these things;
do not ask for that which you ought not.

DOCTRINE AND COVENANTS 8:10

Two centuries ago, Edward Young said that procrastination is the thief of time. Actually, procrastination is much more. It is the thief of our self-respect. It nags at us and spoils our fun. It deprives us of the fullest realization of our ambitions and hopes. Knowing this, we jar ourselves back to reality with the sure knowledge that, "This is my day of opportunity. I will not waste it."

Our attitude, then, is to make the most of our God-given talents. To study, to learn, to achieve, to excel, to prepare for our life's opportunities.

LIFT YOUR EYES HEAVENWARD

As we have therefore opportunity,
let us do good unto all men, especially unto
them who are of the household of faith.

GALATIANS 6:10

No space of regret will make amends for your life's opportunities misused. I bear testimony that regardless of how long you live, your mortal life will be far too short for its vast means of usefulness. I bear testimony that as you lift your eyes heavenward to the star of Christ, as you incorporate within your lives the gospel of Jesus Christ, that light which will come from our Lord will guide you to your opportunity.

HAPPINESS IS FOUND AT HOME

For behold, this is my work and my glory—
to bring to pass the immortality and eternal life of man.

MOSES 1:39

Frequently, frowns outnumber smiles and despair dampens joy. We live so far below the level of our divine possibilities. Some become confused by materialism, entangled by sin, and lost among the passing parade of humanity. Others cry out in the words of the convert of Philip of old: "How can I [find my way], except some man should guide me?" (Acts 8:31).

Happiness does not consist of a glut of luxury, the world's idea of a "good time." Nor must we search for it in faraway places with strange-sounding names. Happiness is found at home.

GOD-GIVEN DIRECTION

Wherefore, I said unto you, feast upon the words of Christ; for behold, the words of Christ will tell you all things what ye should do.

2 NEPHI 32:3

Sacred writ and prophetic revelations provide us knowledge of who we are, from whence we came, and where we shall go when we depart mortality. Baptism, confirmation, priesthood, mission, marriage, and family are more than mere words. To you and to me they are God-given directions for our safe flight.

OPPORTUNITIES IN OUR OWN BACKYARDS

Every man seeking the interest of his neighbor,
and doing all things with an eye single to the glory of God.

DOCTRINE AND COVENANTS 82:19

Too often when we speak of missionary work we think only of faraway places with strange-sounding names and thereby overlook the opportunities to be found in our own backyards.

A Sanctuary from the World

Jesus answered and said unto him,
If a man love me, he will keep my words: and
my Father will love him, and we will come
unto him, and make our abode with him.

JOHN 14:23

More and more the world is filled with chaos and confusion. Messages surround us which contradict all that we hold dear—enticing us to turn from that which is "virtuous, lovely, or of good report or praiseworthy" (Articles of Faith 1:13) and embrace the thinking which often prevails outside the gospel of Jesus Christ. However, when our families are united in purpose, and an atmosphere of peace and love prevails, home becomes a sanctuary from the world. When we are tired or ill or discouraged, how sweet the comfort of being able to turn homeward. We are blessed to belong and to have a place in the family circle.

TRUTH TAUGHT IN BOLDNESS

The Spirit of the Lord God is upon me; because the Lord hath anointed me to preach good tidings unto the meek; he hath sent me to bind up the brokenhearted, to proclaim liberty to the captives, and the opening of the prison to them that are bound.

ISAIAH 61:1

Frustration flees, doubt disappears, and uncertainty wanes when truth is taught in boldness, yet in a spirit of humility by those who have been called to serve the Prince of Peace—even Jesus Christ.

OTHERS WHO HAVE PASSED THIS WAY

Surely he hath borne our griefs,
and carried our sorrows:
yet we did esteem him stricken,
smitten of God, and afflicted.

ISAIAH 53:4

Whenever we are inclined to feel burdened down with the blows of life's fight, let us remember that others have passed the same way, have endured, and then have overcome.

Job was a perfect and an upright man who "feared God, and eschewed evil" (Job 1:1). Pious in his conduct, prosperous in his fortune, Job was to face a test which would tempt any man. Shorn of his possessions, scorned by his friends, afflicted by his suffering, even tempted by his wife, Job was to declare from the depths of his noble soul, "Behold, my witness is in heaven, and my record is on high. . . . I know that my redeemer liveth" (Job 16:19; 19:25).

THREADS OF SERVICE

*For I remember the word of God which
saith by their works ye shall know them; for if their
works be good, then they are good also.*

MORONI 7:5

Woven into the tapestry of your lives are threads of service, of love, of kindness to others. Sometimes you feel inadequate and ineffective because you can't do all that you feel you should. Rather than continually dwelling on what still needs to be done, pause occasionally and reflect on all that you do and have done. It is most significant. The good you have done, the kind words you have spoken, the love you have shown to others, can never be fully measured.

ACTIONS SPEAK LOUDER THAN WORDS

Let us labour therefore
to enter into that rest, lest any man fall
after the same example of unbelief.

HEBREWS 4:11

Years ago we danced to a popular song, the words of which were, "It's easy to say I love you, it's easy to say I'll be true, easy to say these simple things, but prove it by the things you do."

Yes, the oft-repeated statement is yet ever true: "Actions speak louder than words." And the actions whereby we demonstrate that we truly do love God and our neighbor as ourselves will rarely be such as to attract the gaze and admiration of the world. Usually our love will be shown in our day-by-day associations with one another.

THE GREATEST OF FEARS

The Lord said unto him, Who hath made man's mouth? or who maketh the dumb, or deaf, or the seeing, or the blind? have not I the Lord? Now therefore go, and I will be thy mouth, and teach thee what thou shalt say.

EXODUS 4:11–12

Should there be anyone who feels he is too weak to change the onward and downward moving course of his life, or should there be those who fail to resolve to do better because of that greatest of fears, the fear of failure, there is no more comforting assurance to be had than the words of the Lord: "My grace is sufficient for all men that humble themselves before me; for if they humble themselves before me, and have faith in me, then will I make weak things become strong unto them" (Ether 12:27).

A War for the Souls of Mankind

*But whosoever shall deny me
before men, him will I also deny before
my Father which is in heaven.*

MATTHEW 10:33

I am concerned that there is a great war going on for the souls of mankind. We have all known that, but I think we are witnessing it with greater clarity and force than ever before.

We who are on the Lord's side of the ledger have to compete ever more diligently to offset that which is on the devil's side of the ledger.

YOUR LIFE IS
IN YOUR HANDS

*And thou shalt be secure, because there
is hope; yea, thou shalt dig about thee, and
thou shalt take thy rest in safety.*

JOB 11:18

At a large Air Force base, men were taught to jump from high-flying planes, depending for their lives on the parachute each wore. Some died when chutes failed to open. Those who packed them had not been careful. The result was tragedy. Then a solution was devised. Periodically, the base commander would assemble all who had packed the chutes. Each would be handed a parachute he had personally packed. These men would then board a plane and while high in the sky would themselves jump, depending for their lives on the very chute each had packed. The results were gratifying. Not a single death occurred—then or later.

BEGIN IN YOUR OWN FAMILY

Honor thy father and thy mother,
that thy days may be long upon the land
which the Lord thy God giveth thee.

MOSIAH 13:20

There are hearts to gladden. There are deeds to be done. There are souls to be saved. We need not think such opportunities are found only in faraway places. Most will be discovered close at hand. Perhaps we could well begin with our own families. Are we as parents setting before our precious children an example worthy of emulation? Do our actions conform to the teachings of the Master? We can make our houses homes and our homes heavens when the Savior becomes the center of our lives and His example of love and service finds meaningful expression in our own lives.

WISE MEN AND WOMEN OBEY

And we know that all things work together
for good to them that love God, to them who
are the called according to his purpose.

ROMANS 8:28

Answers to our questions and responses to our prayers may come to us through silent promptings of the Spirit. As William Cowper wrote:

> *God moves in a mysterious way*
> *His wonders to perform;*
> *He plants his footsteps in the sea*
> *And rides upon the storm. . . .*
> *Judge not the Lord by feeble sense,*
> *But trust him for his grace;*
> *Behind a frowning providence*
> *He hides a smiling face.*
> (Hymns, *no. 285*)

We watch. We wait. We listen for that still, small voice. When it speaks, we obey.

ONE WHO GOES BEFORE

Remember the days of old, consider the years of many generations: ask thy father, and he will shew thee; thy elders, and they will tell thee.

DEUTERONOMY 32:7

Webster defines a pioneer as "one who goes before, showing others the way to follow." When we go worthily into the house of God and receive our endowments, our sealing blessings, and when we go there regularly to perform work for our kindred dead, we become pioneers, because we literally go before our children and show them the way to follow.

SEPTEMBER

Ask, and it shall be given you;
seek, and ye shall find; knock, and
it shall be opened unto you.

MATTHEW 7:7

LISTEN TO HIM

Learn of me, and listen to my words;
walk in the meekness of my Spirit,
and you shall have peace in me.

DOCTRINE AND COVENANTS 19:23

From time to time the question has been posed, "If Jesus appeared to you today, what questions would you ask of Him?"

My answer has always been, "I would not utter a word. I would listen to Him."

Down through the generations of time, the message from Jesus has been the same. To Peter by the shores of beautiful Galilee, He said, "Follow me." To Philip of old came the call, "Follow me." To Levi who sat at receipt of customs came the instruction, "Follow me." And to you and to me shall come that same beckoning invitation, "Follow me."

You Make a Life by What You Give

*For all these have of their abundance cast in
unto the offerings of God: but she of her penury
hath cast in all the living that she had.*

Luke 21:4

As we view the disillusionment that today
engulfs countless thousands, we are learning
the hard way what an ancient prophet wrote
out for us three thousand years ago: "He that
loveth silver shall not be satisfied with silver;
nor he that loveth abundance with increase"
(Ecclesiastes 5:10).

It is an immutable law that the more you give
away, the more you receive. You make a living
by what you get, but you make a life by what
you give.

THE CAPACITY
TO BECOME LIKE HIM

He said unto them, But whom say ye that I am?
Peter answering said, The Christ of God.

LUKE 9:20

I proffer these three suggestions:

1. Learn of Him. "Learn of me," He pleaded, "for I am meek and lowly in heart: and ye shall find rest unto your souls" (Matthew 11:29).

2. Believe in Him. His is the only name under heaven whereby we might be saved.

3. Follow Him. He brought reality to the word compassion. He showed us the way. He marked the path we should follow. Selfless service characterized His life.

By learning of Him, by believing in Him, by following Him, there is the capacity to become like Him.

THE MIRROR
OF TRUTH

Cast out first the beam out of thine own eye,
and then shalt thou see clearly to pull out
the mote that is in thy brother's eye.

LUKE 6:42

Before we can love and respect our neighbor, we must place him in proper perspective. One man said, "I looked at my brother with the microscope of criticism and I said, 'How coarse my brother is.' I looked at my brother with the telescope of scorn and I said, 'How small my brother is.' Then I looked into the mirror of truth and I said, 'How like me my brother is.'"

Fortified with Truth

They did fast and pray oft, and did wax
stronger and stronger in their humility, and
firmer and firmer in the faith of Christ, unto the
filling their souls with joy and consolation.

Helaman 3:35

It's important that we are fortified with truth, that we might turn our backs to the adversary, that there will be no equivocation, that each man will make up his mind what to say and what to do under any circumstance.

PURPOSEFUL DECISIONS

*He hath given unto you that ye might know
good from evil, and he hath given unto you that ye might
choose life or death; and ye can do good and be restored
unto that which is good, . . . or ye can do evil.*

HELAMAN 14:31

There is no resting place along the path called faithfulness. The trek is constant, and no lingering is allowed. It must not be expected that the road of life spreads itself in an unobstructed view before the person starting his journey. He must anticipate coming upon forks and turnings in the road. But he cannot hope to reach his desired journey's end if he thinks aimlessly about whether to go east or west. He must make decisions purposefully.

A Higher Power

And there appeared an angel unto him
from heaven, strengthening him.

Luke 22:43

In a quiet grove at Valley Forge, there is a heroic-sized monument to George Washington. He is depicted not astride a charging horse nor overlooking a battlefield of glory, but kneeling in humble prayer, calling upon the God of Heaven for divine help. To gaze upon the statue prompts the mind to remember the oft-heard expression, "A man never stands taller than when upon his knees."

Men and women of integrity, character, and purpose have ever recognized a power higher than themselves and have sought through prayer to be guided by that power. Such has it ever been. So shall it ever be.

THE BEST USE OF OUR TIME

Then Jesus said unto them,
My time is not yet come:
but your time is alway ready.

JOHN 7:6

Success is contingent upon our effective use of the time given us. When we cease peering backwards into the mists of our past, and craning forward into the fog that shrouds the future, and concentrate upon doing what lies clearly at hand, then we are making the best and happiest use of our time.

THE LABORATORIES OF OUR LIVES

*Yea, they had been taught by their
mothers, that if they did not doubt,
God would deliver them.*

ALMA 56:47

It is in the home that we form our attitudes, our deeply held beliefs. It is in the home that hope is fostered or destroyed. Our homes are the laboratories of our lives. What we do there determines the course of our lives when we leave home. Dr. Stuart E. Rosenberg wrote in his book *The Road to Confidence,* "Despite all new inventions and modern designs, fads and fetishes, no one has yet invented, or will ever invent, a satisfying substitute for one's own family."

A happy home is but an earlier heaven.

TO FEEL INSPIRATION

Wherefore, stand ye in holy places, and be not moved, until the day of the Lord come; for behold, it cometh quickly, saith the Lord.

DOCTRINE AND COVENANTS 87:8

If you want to see the light of heaven, if you want to feel the inspiration of Almighty God, if you want to have that feeling within your bosom that your Heavenly Father is guiding you to the left or guiding you to the right, follow the instruction from the passage, "Stand ye in holy places and be not moved," and then the spirit of our Heavenly Father will be yours.

A MISSIONARY-MINDED PEOPLE

Behold, verily I say unto you, that it is my will that you should proclaim my gospel from land to land, and from city to city, yea, in those regions round about where it has not been proclaimed.

DOCTRINE AND COVENANTS 66:5

We are a missionary-minded people. We have a divine mandate to proclaim the message of the Restoration. That energetic missionary from the Book of Mormon, even Alma, provides for us a blueprint for missionary conduct: "This is my glory, that perhaps I may be an instrument in the hands of God to bring some soul to repentance; and this is my joy" (Alma 29:9).

DIVINE ATTRIBUTES

*According as his divine power hath given unto us all things
that pertain unto life and godliness, through the knowledge
of him that hath called us to glory and virtue: Whereby
are given unto us exceeding great and precious promises.*

2 PETER 1:3–4

We have been provided divine attributes to guide our journey. We enter mortality not to float with the moving currents of life, but with the power to think, to reason, and to achieve. We left our heavenly home and came to earth in the purity and innocence of childhood.

A PANORAMIC VISION

Where there is no vision, the people perish:
but he that keepeth the law, happy is he.

PROVERBS 29:18

I don't believe that we can be wise without vision. You and I have a responsibility to have that kind of vision which will not be content with one step ahead or two steps ahead; but really to see the end from the beginning, to have a panoramic vision of our opportunities, would be the desire of the heart when one is in tune with the spirit of Christ.

We should realize, when we go abroad in the land to seek our opportunities, that really and truly we are not simply filling a job. We can indeed seek to excel. We can bring credit to the Church. We can be a pillar in the community.

Spiritual Eyesight

Blessed are your eyes, for they see:
and your ears, for they hear.

Matthew 13:16

Those who have felt the touch of the Master's hand somehow cannot explain the change which comes into their lives. There is a desire to live better, to serve faithfully, to walk humbly, and to be more like the Savior. Having received their spiritual eyesight and glimpsed the promises of eternity, they echo the words of the blind man to whom Jesus restored sight: "One thing I know, that, whereas I was blind, now I see" (John 9:25).

FISHERS OF MEN

And Jesus said unto them,
Come ye after me, and I will make
you to become fishers of men.

MARK 1:17

During the Master's ministry, He called fishermen at Galilee to leave their nets and follow Him, declaring, "I will make you fishers of men" (Matthew 4:19). May we join the ranks of the fishers of men and women, that we might provide whatever help we can.

Ours is the duty to reach out to rescue those who have left the safety of activity, that such might be brought to the table of the Lord to feast on His word, to enjoy the companionship of His Spirit, and to be "no more strangers and foreigners, but fellowcitizens with the saints, and of the household of God" (Ephesians 2:19).

"SERVICE WITH A SMILE"

Let us cheerfully do all things that lie in our power;
and then may we stand still, with the utmost assurance, to
see the salvation of God, and for his arm to be revealed.

DOCTRINE AND COVENANTS 123:17

Balanced service is a virtue to be cherished. There is to be time in your life to serve God, to serve your family, to serve your country and community, to serve your employer. "Service with a smile" is far more than a department store slogan. It is a way of life and a path to happiness.

True Finishers

Thou wilt keep him in perfect peace,
whose mind is stayed on thee:
because he trusteth in thee.

Isaiah 26:3

It has been said that the door of history turns on small hinges and so do people's lives. We are constantly making small decisions. The outcome determines the success or failure of our lives. That is why it is worthwhile to look ahead, to set a course, and at least be partly ready when the moment of decision comes. True finishers have the capacity to visualize their objective.

PERSEVERE
AND ENDURE

The natural branches began to grow and thrive
exceedingly; and the wild branches began to be plucked
off and to be cast away; and they did keep the root and
the top thereof equal, according to the strength thereof.

JACOB 5:73

We know that there are times when we will experience heartbreaking sorrow, when we will grieve, and when we may be tested to our limits. However, such difficulties allow us to change for the better, to rebuild our lives in the way our Heavenly Father teaches us, and to become something different from what we were—better than we were, more understanding than we were, more empathetic than we were, with stronger testimonies than we had before.

This should be our purpose—to persevere and endure, yes, but also to become more spiritually refined as we make our way through sunshine and sorrow.

KNOW
FOR YOURSELF

*If any of you lack wisdom, let him
ask of God, that giveth to all men liberally, and
upbraideth not; and it shall be given him.*

JAMES 1:5

In order for us to be strong and to withstand
all the forces pulling us in the wrong direction
or all the voices encouraging us to take the
wrong path, we must have our own testimony.
Whether you are 12 or 112—or anywhere in
between—you can know for yourself that the
gospel of Jesus Christ is true. Read the Book of
Mormon. Ponder its teachings. Ask Heavenly
Father if it is true. We have the promise that "if
ye shall ask with a sincere heart, with real intent, having faith in Christ, he will manifest the
truth of it unto you, by the power of the Holy
Ghost" (Moroni 10:4).

ANTICIPATE THE FUTURE

And ye may know that he is, by the power of the Holy Ghost;
wherefore I would exhort you that ye deny not the power of
God; for he worketh by power, according to the faith of the
children of men, the same today and tomorrow, and forever.

MORONI 10:7

It took man five thousand years to go from the sailboat to the steamboat; a hundred years from the steamboat to the airplane. There were only forty years from the Air Age to the Atomic Age and only twelve years from the Atomic Age to the Space Age.

In the Space Age, the flow of knowledge is as relentless and in a real sense as uncompromising as the spring flow of the rushing waters of the Snake River. It imposes on us the stiff, and in many ways new, requirement that we not merely adjust to, but that we anticipate the future.

WE ARE NEVER ALONE

My help cometh from the Lord,
which made heaven and earth.

PSALM 121:2

In our lives, sickness comes to loved ones, accidents leave their cruel marks of remembrance, and tiny legs that once ran are imprisoned in a wheelchair. There follows the inevitable blaming of oneself, the condemnation of a careless action, and the perennial questions: if, why, where, how. Self-pity, personal withdrawal, or deep despair will not bring peace. Rather, we must go forward, look upward, and rise heavenward. It is imperative that we recognize that whatever has happened to us has happened to others. They have coped and so must we. We are not alone. Heavenly Father's help is near.

Put Your
Hand in His

*Then spake Jesus again unto them, saying, I am
the light of the world: he that followeth me shall not
walk in darkness, but shall have the light of life.*

John 8:12

In this journey called mortality, clouds of gloom may appear on the horizon of our personal destiny. The way ahead may be uncertain, foreboding. In desperation we may be prompted to ask, as did another:

I said to the man who stood at the gate of the year, "Give me a light, that I may tread safely into the unknown."

And he replied, "Go out into the darkness and put your hand into the hand of god.

"That shall be to you better than a light and safer than a known way" (M. Louise Haskins, "The Gate of the Year").

THE GREATEST COMMANDMENT

Jesus said unto him, Thou shalt love the Lord thy God with all thy heart, and with all thy soul, and with all thy mind. This is the first and great commandment. And the second is like unto it, Thou shalt love thy neighbor as thyself.

MATTHEW 22:37–39

Abraham Lincoln accurately described our plight: "We have grown in numbers, wealth, and power as no other nation has ever grown; but we have forgotten God. We have forgotten the gracious hand which preserved us in peace and multiplied and enriched and strengthened us" ("Proclamation to Appoint a National Fast Day," Washington, D.C., March 30, 1864). Can we extricate ourselves from this frightful condition? Is there a way out? If so, what is the way? We can solve this perplexing dilemma by adopting the counsel given by Jesus to the inquiring lawyer who asked, "Master, which is the great commandment in the law?" (Matthew 22:36).

DAILY SPIRITUALITY

*They that were foolish took their lamps,
and took no oil with them: But the wise took
oil in their vessels with their lamps.*

MATTHEW 25:3–4

Spirituality is not like a water faucet that can be turned off or turned on at will. Some make the fatal error of assuming that religion is for others and "perhaps someday for me." Such thinking is not based on fact or experience, for we are daily becoming what we shall be ultimately.

THE GROWTH OF OUR CHARACTER

*And that which fell among thorns are they,
which, when they have heard, go forth, and are
choked with cares and riches and pleasures of
this life, and bring no fruit to perfection.*

LUKE 8:14

Too many have been screaming ever louder for more and more of the things we cannot take with us and paying less and less attention to the real sources of the very happiness we seek. We have been measuring our fellowman more by balance sheets and less by moral standards. We have developed frightening physical power and fallen into pathetic spiritual weakness. We have become so concerned over the growth of our earning capacity that we have neglected the growth of our character.

SACRED SANCTUARY

Therefore are they before the throne of God, and serve him day and night in his temple: and he that sitteth on the throne shall dwell among them.

REVELATION 7:15

The world can be a challenging and difficult place in which to live. We are often surrounded by that which would drag us down. As you and I go to the holy houses of God, as we remember the covenants we make within, we will be more able to bear every trial and to overcome each temptation. In this sacred sanctuary we will find peace; we will be renewed and fortified.

YOUR INFLUENCE FOR GOOD

His lord said unto him, Well done, good and faithful servant; thou hast been faithful over a few things, I will make thee ruler over many things: enter thou into the joy of thy lord.

MATTHEW 25:23

Share your talents. Each of you, single or married, regardless of age, has the opportunity to learn and grow. Expand your knowledge, both intellectual and spiritual, to the full stature of your divine potential. There is no limit to your influence for good. Share your talents, for that which we willingly share, we keep. But that which we selfishly keep, we lose.

A FOUNDATION OF SACRIFICE AND FAITH

Therefore thus saith the Lord God, Behold, I lay in Zion for a foundation a stone, a tried stone, a precious corner stone, a sure foundation: he that believeth shall not make haste.

ISAIAH 28:16

Each of us has a heritage—whether from pioneer forebears, later converts, or others who helped to shape our lives. This heritage provides a foundation built of sacrifice and faith. Ours is the privilege and responsibility to build on such firm and stable footing.

LESSONS FROM THE PAST

Thy speech shall be low out of the dust, and thy voice shall be, as of one that hath a familiar spirit, out of the ground, and thy speech shall whisper out of the dust.

ISAIAH 29:4

Lessons from the past, challenges of the future display dramatically the need for God's help today. Earnestly seek it, and you shall surely find it. Remember that the roads you travel so briskly lead out of dim antiquity, and you study the past chiefly because of its bearing on the living present and its promise for the future. When one fails to learn from the lessons of the past, he is doomed to repeat the same mistakes and suffer their attendant consequences.

THE CAPACITY FOR CREATIVITY

Give instruction to a wise man, and he will be yet wiser: teach a just man, and he will increase in learning.

PROVERBS 9:9

Machines are not creative or imaginative, nor even responsible. They are simply tools, and tools do not work and serve mankind until skilled hands take them up. Because our tools are growing in complexity and in potential usefulness, we must grow in order to use them both profitably and wisely. Let us not be frightened. Rather, let us be challenged. Only the human mind has the capacity for creativity, imagination, insight, vision, and responsibility.

OCTOBER

*The field is white already to harvest;
and lo, he that thrusteth in his
sickle with his might, the same layeth
up in store that he perisheth not,
but bringeth salvation to his soul;
And faith, hope, charity and love, with
an eye single to the glory of God,
qualify him for the work.*

DOCTRINE AND COVENANTS 4:4–5

MORE THAN A TEACHER

A man that hath friends must
shew himself friendly: and there is a friend
that sticketh closer than a brother.

PROVERBS 18:24

Home and visiting teaching are more than mechanical visits once per month. Ours is the responsibility to teach, to inspire, to motivate, and where we visit those who are not active, to bring to activity and to eventual exaltation the sons and daughters of God.

President Ezra Taft Benson urged: "Above all, be a genuine friend to the individuals and families you teach. A friend makes more than a dutiful visit each month. A friend is more concerned about helping people than getting credit. A friend cares. A friend [shows love]. A friend listens, and a friend reaches out" (*Ensign,* May 1987, 50).

THAT OTHERS MIGHT BE LIFTED

If any man serve me, let him follow me; and where I am, there shall also my servant be: if any man serve me, him will my Father honour.

JOHN 12:26

Not only by precept did Jesus teach, but also by example. He was faithful to His divine mission. He stretched forth His hand that others might be lifted toward God.

The beloved apostles noted well His example. He lived not so to be ministered unto, but to minister; not to receive, but to give; not to save His life, but to pour it out for others.

THIS GREAT MISSIONARY CAUSE

How beautiful upon the mountains are the feet of him that bringeth good tidings, that publisheth peace; that bringeth good tidings of good, that publisheth salvation; that saith unto Zion, Thy God reigneth!

ISAIAH 52:7

Let there be no mistake—there is a need for every one of us to be a missionary. Our Lord and Savior has endowed you and me with certain abilities and characteristics. He has made it possible for some missionaries to appeal to certain men, others to appeal to another group. Every holder of the priesthood of God is needed in this great missionary cause.

ENTRUSTED WITH HIS ERRANDS

But there is a spirit in man:
and the inspiration of the Almighty
giveth them understanding.

JOB 32:8

The Lord's purposes are often accomplished as we pay heed to the guidance of the Spirit. I believe that the more we act upon the inspiration and impressions which come to us, the more the Lord will entrust to us His errands.

THE JOY
OF CREATION

Adam began to till the earth, and to have dominion
over all the beasts of the field, and to eat his bread
by the sweat of his brow, as I the Lord had commanded
him. And Eve, also, his wife, did labor with him.

MOSES 5:1

God left the world unfinished for man to work his skill upon. He left the electricity in the cloud, the oil in the earth. He left the rivers unbridged, the forests unfelled and the cities unbuilt. God gives to us the challenge of raw materials, not the ease of finished things. He leaves the pictures unpainted and the music unsung and the problems unsolved, that we might know the joys and glories of creation.

STRIVE TO SERVE

*For I will pour water upon him
that is thirsty, and floods upon the dry
ground: I will pour my spirit upon thy seed,
and my blessing upon thine offspring.*

ISAIAH 44:3

I am reminded of a highly successful business executive in Salt Lake City who served as a counselor in his ward bishopric while at the same time earning his master's degree. During the hectic period preceding finals, the bishop asked him, "Lynn, I know you are facing a crisis in your schooling. Let us relieve you of your meeting schedule and some of the details of your assignments during the next two weeks." Lynn answered, "Bishop, I would ask that rather than relieving me of responsibility, let me assume additional duties. I want to go to the Lord and ask His help by right, not by grace." He never slackened.

Choose the Harder Right

Wherefore, I show unto you the way to judge; for every thing which inviteth to do good, and to persuade to believe in Christ, is sent forth by the power and gift of Christ; wherefore ye may know with a perfect knowledge it is of God.

Moroni 7:16

Signs of national weakness pose threats to our quest for the perfect life—and these threats grow more prevalent as each day goes by. Some of them are:

1. The growing trend toward personal non-involvement;

2. The rising tide of mediocrity; and

3. The choice of security over opportunity.

Refuse to compromise with expedience. Maintain the courage to defy the consensus. Choose the harder right instead of the easier wrong. By so doing, you will not detour, but rather ever remain on the way to perfection.

A HELPING HAND

Serve the Lord with gladness:
come before his presence with singing.

PSALM 100:2

There are men and women everywhere who would be made better by our helping hand. They may be our neighbors, our friends, our business associates. All are our brothers and sisters.

The prayer of my heart is that such persons everywhere will respond to the kind invitation and gentle touch of the Master's hand and faithfully serve our Lord and our Savior, who so willingly died that we might forever live, hopefully having eyes that really see, ears that truly hear, and responsive hearts that know and feel.

THE LIGHTHOUSE
OF THE LORD

*The Lord is my rock, and my fortress, and my
deliverer; my God, my strength, in whom I will trust;
. . . I will call upon the Lord, who is worthy to be
praised: so shall I be saved from mine enemies.*

PSALM 18:2–3

Look to the lighthouse of the Lord. There is
no fog so dense, no night so dark, no gale so
strong, no mariner so lost but what its beacon
light can rescue. It beckons through the storms
of life. The lighthouse of the Lord sends forth
signals readily recognized and never failing.

HE SECURED
OUR SALVATION

Truly my soul waiteth upon God:
from him cometh my salvation.

PSALM 62:1

I believe that none of us can conceive the full import of what Christ did for us in Gethsemane, but I am grateful every day of my life for His atoning sacrifice in our behalf.

At the last moment, He could have turned back. But He did not. He passed beneath all things that He might save all things. In doing so, He gave us life beyond this mortal existence. He reclaimed us from the Fall of Adam.

To the depths of my very soul, I am grateful to Him. He taught us how to live. He taught us how to die. He secured our salvation.

THE PRINCIPLE OF LOVE

Keep yourselves in the love of God, looking for the mercy of our Lord Jesus Christ unto eternal life.

JUDE 1:21

I have found that two fundamental reasons largely account for a return to activity and for changes of attitudes, habits, and actions. First, individuals return because someone has shown them their eternal possibilities and has helped them decide to achieve them. Second, others return because loved ones or "fellowcitizens with the saints" (Ephesians 2:19) have followed the admonition of the Savior, have loved their neighbors as themselves, and have helped others to bring their dreams to fulfillment and their ambitions to realization.

The catalyst in this process has been—and will continue to be—the principle of love.

FIRST COMES
THE TEST OF FAITH

Jesus answered and said unto them, Verily I say unto you, If ye have faith, and doubt not, ye shall not only do this which is done to the fig tree, but also if ye shall say unto this mountain, Be thou removed, and be thou cast into the sea; it shall be done.

MATTHEW 21:21

It was not raining when Noah was commanded to build an ark. Two Heavenly Personages were not yet seen when Joseph knelt and prayed. There was no visible ram in the thicket when Abraham prepared to sacrifice his son Isaac. First came the test of faith, and then the miracle.

Remember that faith and doubt cannot exist in the same mind at the same time, for one will dispel the other. Cast out doubt. Cultivate faith. Strive always to retain that childlike faith which can move mountains and bring heaven closer to heart and home.

LISTENING TO TRULY UNDERSTAND

*Keep therefore and do them; for this is your wisdom
and your understanding in the sight of the nations,
which shall hear all these statutes, and say, Surely this
great nation is a wise and understanding people.*

DEUTERONOMY 4:6

Listening is not a passive activity. To actively listen to another person requires willpower, concentration, and great mental effort. Its rewards are great, because only then do you really learn to understand.

HE WHO
KNOWS US BEST

And the peace of God, which passeth all understanding,
shall keep your hearts and minds through Christ Jesus.

PHILIPPIANS 4:7

We were not placed on this earth to walk alone. What an amazing source of power, of strength, and of comfort is available to each of us. He who knows us better than we know ourselves, He who sees the larger picture and who knows the end from the beginning, has assured us that He will be there for us to provide help if we but ask. We have the promise: "Pray always, and be believing, and all things shall work together for your good" (Doctrine and Covenants 90:24).

STRIVE
FOR PERFECTION

*Therefore I would that ye should be perfect even as
I, or your Father who is in heaven is perfect.*

3 NEPHI 12:48

Our goal is to achieve, to excel, to strive for perfection. Remember, however, that our business in life is not to get ahead of others but to get ahead of ourselves. To break our own record, to outstrip our yesterdays by today, to bear our trials more beautifully than we ever dreamed we could, to give as we never have given, to do our work with more force and a finer finish than ever—this is the true objective. And to accomplish this task, our attitude is reflected in a determination to make the most of our opportunities.

Discover Peace

But thou, when thou prayest, enter into thy closet, and when thou hast shut thy door, pray to thy Father which is in secret; and thy Father which seeth in secret shall reward thee openly.

Matthew 6:6

This guiding instruction has helped troubled souls discover the peace for which they fervently yearn and earnestly hope.

Unfortunately, prosperity, abundance, honor, and praise lead some men to the false security of haughty self-assurance and the abandonment of the inclination to pray. Conversely, trial, tribulation, sickness, and death crumble the castles of men's pride and bring them to their knees to petition for power from on high.

THE GLORY
WE SEEK

*There is one glory of the sun, and another glory of the moon,
and another glory of the stars: for one star differeth from
another star in glory. So also is the resurrection of the dead.*

1 CORINTHIANS 15:41–42

It is the celestial glory which we seek. It is in
the presence of God we desire to dwell. It is a
forever family in which we want membership.
Such blessings must be earned.

Where did we come from? Why are we here?
Where do we go after this life? No longer need
these universal questions remain unanswered.
Our Heavenly Father rejoices for those who
keep His commandments. Tenderly the Master
speaks to all: "Come back. Come home. Come
unto me." What eternal joy awaits when we accept His divine invitation to exaltation.

PATHWAY TO THE ABUNDANT LIFE

And they were called the people of God.
And the Lord did pour out his Spirit upon them, and
they were blessed, and prospered in the land.

MOSIAH 25:24

Since this is a day of the ready reference, the condensed version, the handy guide, may I offer brief suggestions—even steps—for your pathway to the abundant life:

Step 1. Labor to learn.

Step 2. Strive to serve.

Step 3. Think to thank.

Step 4. Pause to pray.

A Light and a Way

Behold, I am Jesus Christ, the Son of God.
I am the life and the light of the world.

DOCTRINE AND COVENANTS 11:28

Out of Nazareth and down through the generations of time come His excellent example, His welcome words, His divine deeds.

They inspire patience to endure affliction, strength to bear grief, courage to face death, and confidence to meet life. In this world of chaos, of trial, of uncertainty, never has our need for such divine guidance been more desperate.

Lessons from Nazareth, Capernaum, Jerusalem, Galilee transcend the barriers of distance, the passage of time, the limits of understanding, and bring to troubled hearts a light and a way.

ON THE LORD'S ERRAND

And how shall they preach, except they be sent? as it is written, How beautiful are the feet of them that preach the gospel of peace, and bring glad tidings of good things!

ROMANS 10:15

Now, some of you may be shy by nature or consider yourselves inadequate to respond affirmatively to a calling. Remember that this work is not yours and mine alone. It is the Lord's work, and when we are on the Lord's errand, we are entitled to the Lord's help. Remember that the Lord will shape the back to bear the burden placed upon it.

WE NEED NOT STAND ALONE

*And the work of righteousness
shall be peace; and the effect of righteousness
quietness and assurance for ever.*

ISAIAH 32:17

Many members of Relief Society do not have husbands. Death, divorce, and indeed lack of opportunity to marry have, in many instances, made it necessary for a woman to stand alone. In reality, she need not stand alone, for a loving Heavenly Father will be by her side to give direction to her life and provide peace and assurance in those quiet moments where loneliness is found and where compassion is needed.

BALANCE IS KEY

*See that all these things are done in wisdom and order;
for it is not requisite that a man should run faster than
he has strength. And again, it is expedient that he should
be diligent, that thereby he might win the prize.*

<small>MOSIAH 4:27</small>

Balance is key to us in our sacred and solemn responsibilities in our homes and in our Church callings. We must use wisdom, inspiration, and sound judgment as we care for our families and fulfill our Church callings, for each is vitally important. We cannot neglect our families; we must not neglect our Church callings.

THE SERVICE
THAT COUNTS

*This is a faithful saying, and these things I will that
thou affirm constantly, that they which have believed
in God might be careful to maintain good works.
These things are good and profitable unto men.*

TITUS 3:8

While driving to the office one morning, I
passed a dry-cleaning establishment which had
a sign by the side of the front door. It read, "It's
the Service That Counts." I suppose in a highly
competitive field such as the dry-cleaning business
and many others, the differentiating factor
which distinguishes one store from another is,
in actual fact, service.

The message from the small sign simply would
not leave my mind. Suddenly I realized why.
In actual fact it is the service that counts—the
Lord's service.

THE MEASURE OF LIFE

*And whosoever liveth and believeth
in me shall never die.*

JOHN 11:26

We understand we have come to earth to learn, to live, to progress in our eternal journey toward perfection. Some remain on earth but for a moment, while others live long upon the land. The measure is not how long we live, but rather how well we live.

OUR HOME PORT

I have taught thee in the way of wisdom;
I have led thee in right paths.

PROVERBS 4:11

God gave man life, and with it, the power to think, to reason, to decide, and to love. Like the vital rudder of a ship, we have been provided a way to determine the direction we travel. The lighthouse of the Lord beckons to all as we sail the seas of life. Our home port is the celestial kingdom of God. Our purpose is to steer an undeviating course in that direction. A man without a purpose is like a ship without a rudder—never likely to reach home port. To us comes the signal: Chart your course, set your sail, position your rudder, and proceed.

TO TRULY SEE

For this people's heart is waxed gross, and their ears are dull of hearing, and their eyes they have closed; lest at any time they should see with their eyes, and hear with their ears, and should understand with their heart.

MATTHEW 13:15

When Jesus walked and taught among men, He spoke frequently of having hearts that could know and feel, ears that were capable of hearing, and eyes that could truly see.

Each of us knows those who do not have sight. We also know many others who have their eyesight but who walk in darkness at noonday. Some have been blinded by anger; others by indifference, by revenge, by hate, by prejudice, by ignorance, by neglect of precious opportunities.

A SIGNAL THROUGH THE STORM

Rejoice not against me, O mine enemy:
when I fall, I shall arise; when I sit in darkness,
the Lord shall be a light unto me.

MICAH 7:8

Look to the lighthouse of the Lord. There is no fog so dense, no night so dark, no gale so strong, no mariner so lost but what its beacon light can rescue. It beckons through the storms of life. The lighthouse of the Lord sends forth signals readily recognized and never failing.

MAKE A HAPPY LIFE

A merry heart maketh a cheerful countenance:
but by sorrow of the heart the spirit is broken.

PROVERBS 15:13

The happy life is not ushered in at any age to the sound of drums and trumpets. It grows upon us year by year, little by little, until at last we realize that we have it. It is achieved in individuals, not by flights to the moon or Mars, but by a body of work done so well that we can lift our heads with assurance and look the world in the eye. Of this be sure: You do not find the happy life—you make it.

EVERYTHING WE NEED

Ye have not chosen me, but I have chosen you, and ordained you, that ye should go and bring forth fruit, and that your fruit should remain: that whatsoever ye shall ask of the Father in my name, he may give it you.

JOHN 15:16

Each of us has come to this earth with all the tools necessary to make correct choices. The prophet Mormon tells us, "The Spirit of Christ is given to every man, that he may know good from evil" (Moroni 7:16).

We are surrounded—even at times bombarded—by the messages of the adversary. Listen to some of them; they are no doubt familiar to you: "Just this once won't matter." "Don't worry; no one will know." The lies are endless. Although in our journey we will encounter forks and turnings in the road, we simply cannot afford the luxury of a detour from which we may never return.

PUT IT TO THE TEST

I would exhort you that ye would ask God, the Eternal Father, in the name of Christ, if these things are not true; and if ye shall ask with a sincere heart, with real intent, having faith in Christ, he will manifest the truth of it unto you.

MORONI 10:4

Each one of us has the responsibility to find out for himself whether or not this gospel of Jesus Christ is true. If we read the Book of Mormon, read the standard works, and put the teachings to the test, then we shall know of the doctrine, whether it be of man or whether it be of God, for this is our promise.

A BRIGHTER SMILE
THROUGH SERVICE

For I was an hungred, and ye gave me meat:
I was thirsty, and ye gave me drink:
I was a stranger, and ye took me in.

MATTHEW 25:35

God bless all who endeavor to be their brother's keeper, who give to ameliorate suffering, who strive with all that is good within them to make a better world. Have you noticed that such individuals have a brighter smile? Their footsteps are more certain. They have an aura about them of contentment and satisfaction, even dedication, for one cannot participate in helping others without experiencing a rich blessing himself.

November

*If thou art merry, praise the Lord
with singing, with music, with dancing, and
with a prayer of praise and thanksgiving.*

DOCTRINE AND COVENANTS 136:28

HIS CONSTANT
TRUTH PREVAILS

Depart from evil, and do good;
seek peace, and pursue it.

PSALM 34:14

We turn backward in time that we might go forward with hope. Back, back beyond the Space Age, the Computer Age, and Industrial Age. Back, back to Him who walked the dusty paths of villages we now reverently call the Holy Land, to Him who caused the blind to see, the deaf to hear, the lame to walk, and the dead to live. To Him who tenderly and lovingly assured us. "I am the way, the truth, and the life" (John 14:6).

His constant truths prevail in these changing times. His words and those of His Apostles stand forth as rays of hope penetrating the dullness of despair.

THE PRAYER OF A YOUNG MAN

*I at length came to the determination to
"ask of God," concluding that if he gave wisdom
to them that lacked wisdom, and would give
liberally, and not upbraid, I might venture.*

JOSEPH SMITH—HISTORY 1:13

A boy, born in the year of our Lord one thousand eight hundred and five, on the twenty-third of December, in the town of Sharon, Windsor County, State of Vermont, paused to pray that bright day in the grove near Palmyra. Who can calculate the far-reaching effects of that one prayer by the one boy? Do you pause to pray?

A TEST FOR EVERY DECISION

*And as for me, thou upholdest me in mine integrity,
and settest me before thy face for ever.*

PSALM 41:12

Make every decision pass the test:

What does it do to me?

What does it do for me?

And let our code emphasize not "What will others think?" but rather, "What will I think of myself?" Then our Father can say of us as Jesus said of Nathanael, "Behold an Israelite indeed, in whom is no guile!" (John 1:47).

DECLARE YOUR WITNESS

For, for this intent have we written these things, that they may know that we knew of Christ, and we had a hope of his glory many hundred years before his coming.

<small>JACOB 4:4</small>

Lift up your voices and testify to the true nature of the Godhead. Declare your witness concerning the Book of Mormon. Convey the glorious and beautiful truths contained in the plan of salvation.

Your Own Road to Jericho

But a certain Samaritan, as he journeyed,
came where he was: and when he
saw him, he had compassion on him.

Luke 10:33

Each of us, in the journey through mortality, will travel his own Jericho Road. What will be your experience? What will be mine? Will I fail to notice him who has fallen among thieves and requires my help? Will you?

Will I be one who sees the injured and hears his plea, yet crosses to the other side? Will you?

Or will I be one who sees, who hears, who pauses, and who helps? Will you?

Jesus provided our watchword, "Go, and do thou likewise." When we obey that declaration, there opens to our eternal view a vista of joy seldom equaled and never surpassed.

STAND FOR WHAT WE BELIEVE

Fear thou not; for I am with thee: be not dismayed; for I am thy God: I will strengthen thee; yea, I will help thee; yea, I will uphold thee with the right hand of my righteousness.

ISAIAH 41:10

In Lehi's vision of the tree of life, found in 1 Nephi 8, Lehi sees, among others, those who hold to the iron rod until they come forth and partake of the fruit of the tree of life, which we know is a representation of the love of God. And then, sadly, after they partake of the fruit, some are ashamed because of those in the "great and spacious building," who represent the pride of the children of men, who are pointing fingers at them and scoffing at them; and they fall away into forbidden paths and are lost (see 1 Nephi 8:26–28). What a powerful tool of the adversary is ridicule and mockery! Do we have the courage to stand strong and firm?

A DIVINE INVITATION

What man of you, having an hundred sheep, if he lose one of them, doth not leave the ninety and nine in the wilderness, and go after that which is lost, until he find it?

LUKE 15:4

Our Heavenly Father rejoices for those who keep His commandments. He is concerned also for the lost child, the tardy teenager, the wayward youth, the delinquent parent. Tenderly He speaks to these, and indeed to all: "Come back. Come up. Come in. Come home. Come unto me." I pray all mankind may accept His divine invitation to exaltation.

ENJOY LIFE

*The Lord thy God in the midst of thee is mighty;
he will save, he will rejoice over thee with joy; he will
rest in his love, he will joy over thee with singing.*

ZEPHANIAH 3:17

Let us relish life as we live it, find joy in the journey and share our love with friends and family. One day, each of us will run out of tomorrows. Let us not put off what is most important.

THE WAY BACK

Behold, he who has repented of his sins, the same is forgiven, and I, the Lord, remember them no more. By this ye may know if a man repenteth of his sins— behold, he will confess them and forsake them.

DOCTRINE AND COVENANTS 58:42–43

If any has stumbled in his or her journey, I promise you that there is a way back. The process is called repentance. Our Savior died to provide you and me that blessed gift. Though the path is difficult, the promise is real. Said the Lord: "Though your sins be as scarlet, they shall be as white as snow" (Isaiah 1:18). "And I will remember [them] no more" (Jeremiah 31:34).

THE NEED FOR CHARITY

*Except ye have charity ye can in nowise
be saved in the kingdom of God.*

MORONI 10:21

There is a serious need for the charity that
gives attention to those who are unnoticed,
hope to those who are discouraged, aid to those
who are afflicted. True charity is love in action.
The need for charity is everywhere.

Needed is the charity which refuses to find satisfaction in hearing or in repeating the reports
of misfortunes that come to others, unless by so
doing, the unfortunate one may be benefited.
The American educator and politician Horace
Mann once said, "To pity distress is but human; to relieve it is godlike."

A TRADITION OF OBEDIENCE

And behold, all that he requires of you is to keep his commandments; and he has promised you that if ye would keep his commandments ye should prosper in the land; and he never doth vary from that which he hath said.

MOSIAH 2:22

I would hope that every one of us would have a tradition of obedience in his or her life, because all of the blessings of God are predicated upon obedience to the commandments. As we live the commandments, we shall find the answers to our prayers and receive direction in our lives. We will have to put the Lord to the test by following His command, by living the principle, and then we shall receive the reward.

YOUR ETERNAL POSSIBILITIES

For my thoughts are not your thoughts,
neither are your ways my ways, saith the Lord.

ISAIAH 55:8

A patriarchal blessing is a revelation to the recipient, even a white line down the middle of the road, to protect, inspire, and motivate activity and righteousness. A patriarchal blessing literally contains chapters from your book of eternal possibilities. I say eternal, for just as life is eternal, so is a patriarchal blessing. What may not come to fulfillment in this life may occur in the next. We do not govern God's timetable.

THE LIGHT WHICH BRINGS HAPPINESS

And the King shall answer and say unto them,
Verily I say unto you, Inasmuch as ye have done it unto one
of the least of these my brethren, ye have done it unto me.

MATTHEW 25:40

Your service to God and to your fellowmen will not be restricted to the pulpit, the classroom, or your home or visiting teaching visits. Your own personal influence and demonstration of service to God can be the light which brings happiness into the lives of others.

SEEKING EXCELLENCE

But covet earnestly the best gifts:
and yet shew I unto you a more excellent way.

1 CORINTHIANS 12:31

As we strive for perfection, we seek excellence. Excellence may leave you sensitive in the face of the jaded; curious in the crowd of uninterested; quiet in groups of static and noise; caring in the company of the unconcerned; exact while all about you is approximation; refined in place of gross; exceptional instead of commonplace.

CROSSING THE GREAT DEEP

*My son, keep my words, and lay up
my commandments with thee.*

PROVERBS 7:1

I am reminded of the words of the Lord found in the book of Ether in the Book of Mormon. Said the Lord, "Ye cannot cross this great deep save I prepare you against the waves of the sea, and the winds which have gone forth, and the floods which shall come" (Ether 2:25). My brothers and sisters, He has prepared us. If we heed His words and live the commandments we will survive this time of permissiveness and wickedness—a time which can be compared with the waves and the winds and the floods that can destroy. He is ever mindful of us. He loves us and will bless us as we do what is right.

WISDOM
IN BALANCE

A false balance is abomination to the Lord:
but a just weight is his delight.

PROVERBS 11:1

I would like to testify that it's a wise person who knows how to have balance in his life. There's time for business, there's time for family, there's time for spouse, there's time for self, there's time for Christ. We need to have this kind of balance if we are to find wisdom and hence be successful.

AM I MY BROTHER'S KEEPER?

And the Lord said unto Cain:
Where is Abel, thy brother?
And he said: I know not.
Am I my brother's keeper?

MOSES 5:34

Frequently we learn of terrible human suffering as a result of tornadoes, floods, fires, drought, hurricanes, earthquakes, conflicts of war. I ask the question: Do we have a responsibility to do something about such suffering? Long years ago a similar question was posed and preserved in Holy Writ: "And Cain talked with Abel his brother: and it came to pass, when they were in the field, that Cain rose up against Abel his brother, and slew him. And the Lord said unto Cain, Where is Abel thy brother? And he said, I know not: Am I my brother's keeper?" (Genesis 4:8–9) The answer to that vital question is: Yes, we are our brothers' keepers.

IN WHOM
WE TRUST

Trust in the Lord with all thine heart;
and lean not unto thine own understanding.
In all thy ways acknowledge him,
and he shall direct thy paths.

PROVERBS 3:5–6

Be honest with yourself; be honest with others; be honest with God. Then you will acquire what the eminent English statesman William H. Gladstone described as the world's greatest need: "A living faith in a personal God." And in this personal God, our Heavenly Father, we place our trust. As the psalmist wrote ever so long ago: "It is better to trust in the Lord than to put confidence in man. It is better to trust in the Lord than to put confidence in princes" (Psalm 118:8–9).

AN UNFAILING GUIDE

The willing and obedient shall eat the good
of the land of Zion in these last days.

DOCTRINE AND COVENANTS 64:34

There is no need for you or for me, in this enlightened age when the fulness of the gospel has been restored, to sail uncharted seas or to travel unmarked roads in search of truth. A loving Heavenly Father has plotted our course and provided an unfailing guide—even obedience.

WORTHY TO ANSWER THE CALL

Pure religion and undefiled before God and the Father is this, To visit the fatherless and widows in their affliction, and to keep himself unspotted from the world.

JAMES 1:27

Ours is the responsibility to so conduct our lives that when the call comes to provide a priesthood blessing or to assist in any way, we are worthy to do so. We have been told that truly we cannot escape the effect of our personal influence. We must be certain that our influence is positive and uplifting. Are our hands clean? Are our hearts pure?

THE PURE LOVE OF CHRIST

But charity is the pure love of Christ, and it endureth forever; and whoso is found possessed of it at the last day, it shall be well with him.

MORONI 7:47

Life is perfect for none of us. Rather than being judgmental and critical of each other, may we have the pure love of Christ for our fellow travelers in this journey through life. May we recognize that each one is doing his or her best to deal with the challenges which come his or her way, and may we strive to do *our* best to help out.

An Abiding Faith

And having this confidence,
I know that I shall abide and continue with you
all for your furtherance and joy of faith.

Philippians 1:25

Amidst the confusion of our age, the conflicts of conscience, and the turmoil of daily living, an abiding faith becomes an anchor to our lives.

When you have an abiding faith in the living God, when your outward actions reflect your inner convictions, you have the composite strength of exposed and hidden virtues. They combine to give safe passage through whatever rough seas might arise.

THE REACH OF A TESTIMONY

But there was one among them whose name
was Alma, he also being a descendant of Nephi.
And he was a young man, and he believed
the words which Abinadi had spoken.

MOSIAH 17:2

We really don't know how much good we can do until we put forth the effort to achieve our objectives. Our testimonies can penetrate the hearts of others and can bring to them the blessings which will prevail in this troubled world and which will guide them to exaltation.

THE TRUE DEFINITION OF CHARACTER

*God forbid that I should justify you: till I die
I will not remove mine integrity from me. My
righteousness I hold fast, and will not let it go: my
heart shall not reproach me so long as I live.*

JOB 27:5–6

Perhaps the word "character" best describes one who is true to himself. For character takes no account of what you are thought to be, but what you are. Character is having an inner light and the courage to follow its dictates.

One who is true to himself develops the attributes needed to survive errors, to keep marching on a road that seems to be without end, and to rise above disappointment and distress.

HE IS ALWAYS
WITH US

Come unto me, all ye that labour and
are heavy laden, and I will give you rest.

MATTHEW 11:28

Only the Master knows the depths of our trials, our pain, and our suffering. He alone offers us eternal peace in times of adversity. He alone touches our tortured souls with His comforting words:

"Come unto me, all ye that labour and are heavy laden, and I will give you rest" (Matthew 11:28).

Whether it is the best of times or the worst of times, He is with us. He has promised that this will never change.

THE NOBLEST OF VIRTUES

Take upon you the name of Christ; that ye humble yourselves even to the dust, and worship God, in whatsoever place ye may be in, in spirit and in truth; and that ye live in thanksgiving daily.

ALMA 34:38

This is a wonderful time to be on earth. While there is much that is wrong in the world today, there are many things that are right and good. There are marriages that make it, parents who love their children and sacrifice for them, friends who care about us and help us, teachers who teach. Our lives are blessed in countless ways.

We can lift ourselves and others as well when we refuse to remain in the realm of negative thought and cultivate within our hearts an attitude of gratitude. If ingratitude be numbered among the serious sins, then gratitude takes its place among the noblest of virtues.

THE POWER OF CLEAN THOUGHTS

Commit thy works unto the Lord,
and thy thoughts shall be established.

PROVERBS 16:3

President David O. McKay advised, "I implore you to think clean thoughts." He then made this significant declaration of truth: "Every action is preceded by a thought. If we want to control our actions, we must control our thinking."

Fill your minds with good thoughts, and your actions will be proper. May each one of you be able to echo in truth the line from Tennyson spoken by Sir Galahad: "My strength is as the strength of ten, because my heart is pure" (*Familiar Quotations*, 647).

ETERNAL OPPORTUNITIES

*Remember me, O Lord, with the
favour that thou bearest unto thy people:
O visit me with thy salvation.*

PSALM 106:4

Vicarious work performed in our temples must be carried forth in the same spirit of selfless devotion and sacrifice that characterized the life of the Master. When we remember Him, it becomes easier for us to do our individual parts in this vital work. Each time we gaze upon one of these holy houses, may we be reminded of the eternal opportunities which are found inside, not only for ourselves, but for our dead. Let us be mindful that decisions pertaining to the temple are eternal decisions with eternal consequences.

PRAYERS OF FAITH

And also the Lord will remember
the prayers of the righteous, which have
been put up unto him for them.

MORMON 5:21

As we offer unto God our family prayers and our personal prayers, let us do so with faith and trust in Him. If any of us has been slow to hearken to the counsel to pray always, there is no finer hour to begin than now. Those who feel that prayer might denote a physical weakness should remember that a man never stands taller than when he is upon his knees.

IN THE PURSUIT
OF PERFECTION

Out of Zion, the perfection of beauty,
God hath shined.

PSALM 50:2

As we face the temptations of our times, the confusion of choice, the embarrassment of error, the pursuit of perfection, our Heavenly Father is there to listen, to love, to inspire. Our Father to whom we earnestly pray is not an ethereal substance or a mysterious or incomprehensible being. Rather, He has eyes with which to view our actions, lips with which to speak to us, ears to hear our plea, and a heart to understand our love.

DECEMBER

And we talk of Christ, we rejoice in Christ,
we preach of Christ, we prophesy of Christ,
and we write according to our prophecies,
that our children may know to what source
they may look for a remission of their sins.

2 NEPHI 25:26

Jesus of Nazareth

And he came and dwelt in a city called Nazareth:
that it might be fulfilled which was spoken by the
prophets, He shall be called a Nazarene.

Matthew 2:23

Nazareth was situated on the main trade route which ran from Damascus through the Galilean cities to the Mediterranean coast. This, however, was not to be the village's claim to fame. Nor was its glory to be found in the beauty of its environs. Nazareth was the scene of more lasting events and profound consequence than routes of trade or landscapes of beauty. To a city of Galilee, called Nazareth, came the angel Gabriel. To a virgin whose name was Mary, he declared, "Fear not, Mary: for thou hast found favour with God. And, behold, thou shalt conceive in thy womb, and bring forth a son, and shalt call his name Jesus" (Luke 1:30–31).

WE ARE ALL TEACHERS

And thou shalt teach them ordinances and laws, and shalt shew them the way wherein they must walk, and the work that they must do.

EXODUS 18:20

We are all teachers. We should ever remember that we not only teach with words; we teach also by who we are and how we live our lives. As we teach others, may we follow the example of the perfect teacher, our Lord and Savior Jesus Christ. He left His footprints in the sands of the seashore, but left His teaching principles in the hearts and in the lives of all whom He taught. He instructed His disciples of that day, and to us He speaks the same words, "Follow thou me." May we go forward in the spirit of obedient response, that it may be said of each of us as it was spoken of the Redeemer, "Thou art a teacher come from God" (John 3:2).

MAKING CHRISTMAS REAL

There was no darkness in all that night, but it was as light as though it was mid-day. And . . . the sun did rise in the morning again, according to its proper order; and they knew that it was the day that the Lord should be born.

3 NEPHI 1:19

We must make Christmas real. It isn't just tinsel and ribbon, unless we have made it so in our lives. Christmas is the spirit of giving without a thought of getting. It is happiness because we see joy in people. It is forgetting self and finding time for others. It is discarding the meaningless and stressing the true values. It is peace because we have found peace in the Savior's teachings. It is the time we realize most deeply that the more love is expended, the more there is of it for others.

"THE GREAT REFUSAL"

*And, behold, one came and said
unto him, Good Master, what good thing
shall I do, that I may have eternal life?*

MATTHEW 19:16

Our beloved Savior beacons us to follow Him. The choice is ours. You will recall the rich, young ruler who asked the Savior what he should do to have eternal life and, when told to sell his possessions and give to the poor, "went away sorrowful: for he had great possessions" (see Matthew 19:16–22). He preferred the comforts of earth to the treasures of heaven. He would not purchase the things of eternity by abandoning those of time. He made, as Dante calls it, "the great refusal." And so he vanishes from the gospel history, nor do the evangelists know anything of him further. His riches and many possessions had become his God.

OUR CHRISTMAS GIFT LIST

The light and the Redeemer of the world; the Spirit of truth, who came into the world, because the world was made by him, and in him was the life of men and the light of men.

DOCTRINE AND COVENANTS 93:9

Christmas is the time when the bonds of family love transcend distance and inconvenience. It is a time when love of neighbor rises above petty day-to-day irritations, and doors swing open to give and receive expressions of appreciation and affection.

If to our Christmas gift list is added the gift of service—not only to friends and family, but also those who badly need help—then our giving can be complete.

HAVENS OF LOVE

He brought me to the banqueting house,
and his banner over me was love.

SONG OF SOLOMON 2:4

I love the words found in the hymn:

O home belov'd, where'er I wander,
On foreign land or distant sea,
As time rolls by, my heart grows fonder
And yearns more lovingly for thee!
Tho fair be nature's scenes around me,
And friends are ever kind and true,
Tho joyous mirth and song surround me,
My heart, my soul still yearns for you.
("O Home Beloved," Hymns, no. 337.)

May we ever strive to make of our homes havens of love and peace and happiness, where the Spirit of the Lord would choose to dwell.

LET IT BE A SPECIAL TIME

When they saw the star,
they rejoiced with exceeding great joy.

MATTHEW 2:10

As Christmas comes, let it be a time that lights the eyes of children and puts laughter on their lips. Let it be a time for lifting the lives of those who live in loneliness. Let it be a time for calling our families together, for feeling a closeness to those who are near to us and a closeness also to those who are absent. `Let it be a time of prayers for peace, for the preservation of free principles, and for the protection of those who are far from us. Let it be a time of forgetting self and finding time for others. Let it be a time for discarding the meaningless and for stressing the true values. Let it be a time of peace because we have found peace in His teachings.

TEACH AND TESTIFY

*This is the disciple which testifieth
of these things, and wrote these things: and
we know that his testimony is true.*

JOHN 21:24

Regarding your testimony, remember, that which you willingly share you keep, while that which you selfishly keep you lose. Have the courage and the kindness, as did Jesus, to teach those whom you may meet that baptism is essential to salvation. Teach and testify. There is no better combination.

Time to Rededicate

Let your light so shine before men,
that they may see your good works, and
glorify your Father which is in heaven.

Matthew 5:16

There is no better time than now, this very Christmas season, for all of us to rededicate ourselves to the principles taught by Jesus Christ.

Because He came to earth, we have a perfect example to follow. As we strive to become more like Him, we will have joy and happiness in our lives and peace each day of the year. It is His example which, if followed, stirs within us more kindness and love, more respect and concern for others.

GLADDEN LIVES AND TOUCH HEARTS

*Shouldest not thou also have had compassion
on thy fellowservant, even as I had pity on thee?*

MATTHEW 18:33

One evening at Christmastime, my wife and I visited a nursing home. We looked for a 95-year-old widow. As I reached to take her hand, she withdrew it. I noticed that she held firmly to a Christmas greeting card. The attendant smiled and said, "I don't know who sent that card, but she will not lay it aside. She doesn't speak but pats the card and holds it to her lips and kisses it." I recognized the card. It was one my wife, Frances, had sent the week before.

We need not wait for Christmas; we need not postpone till Thanksgiving Day our response to the Savior's tender admonition: "Go, and do thou likewise" (Luke 10:37).

THE VALUE
OF WORK

For thou shalt eat the labour of thine hands:
happy shalt thou be, and it shall be well with thee.

PSALM 128:2

Work is basic to all we do. God's first direction to Adam in the Garden of Eden, as recorded in scripture, was to dress the garden and take care of it. After the fall of Adam, God cursed the earth for Adam's sake, saying, "In the sweat of thy face shalt thou eat bread, till thou return unto the ground" (Genesis 3:19). Today many have forgotten the value of work.

THE SPIRIT OF CHRISTMAS

And the angel said unto them, Fear not: for, behold,
I bring you good tidings of great joy, which shall be
to all people. For unto you is born this day in the city
of David a Saviour, which is Christ the Lord.

LUKE 2:10–11

Probably no other time of the year yields as many poignant memories as does Christmas. The Christmases we remember best generally have little to do with worldly goods, but a lot to do with families, with love, and with compassion and caring. This thought provides hope for those of us who fear that the simple meaning of the holiday is diluted by commercialism, or by opposition from those with differing religious views, or just by getting so caught up in the pressures of the season that we lose that special spirit we could otherwise experience.

AVOIDING REGRETS

Watch ye therefore: for ye know not when the master of the house cometh, at even, or at midnight, or at the cockcrowing, or in the morning: Lest coming suddenly he find you sleeping.

MARK 13:35–36

Send that note to the friend you've been neglecting; give your child a compliment and a hug; say "I love you" more; always express your thanks. Never let a problem to be solved become more important than a person to be loved. Friends move away, children grow up, loved ones pass on. It's so easy to take others for granted, until that day when they're gone from our lives and we are left with feelings of "what if" and "if only."

A REFLECTION OF LOVE AND SELFLESSNESS

*Therefore the Lord himself shall give you a
sign; Behold, a virgin shall conceive, and bear
a son, and shall call his name Immanuel.*

ISAIAH 7:14

Our celebration of Christmas should be
a reflection of the love and selflessness taught
by the Savior. Giving, not getting, brings to
full bloom the Christmas spirit. We feel more
kindly one to another. We reach out in love
to help those less fortunate. Our hearts are
softened. Enemies are forgiven, friends re-
membered, and God obeyed. The spirit of
Christmas illuminates the picture window of
the soul, and we look out upon the world's busy
life and become more interested in people than
in things. To catch the real meaning of the
spirit of Christmas, we need only drop the last
syllable, and it becomes the Spirit of Christ.

A WONDERFUL TIME OF YEAR

And this shall be a sign
unto you; Ye shall find the babe wrapped in
swaddling clothes, lying in a manger.

LUKE 2:12

Christmas is a wonderful time of year. It is a season when there are more smiles, more cheerful greetings, more acts of thoughtful kindness, more sweet remembrances of cherished friends and loved ones than are found through the rest of the entire year. In the troubled times in which we live, this is truly a miracle.

What is it that brings such love into our hearts, such joy into our lives? It is, of course, the spirit of Christmas. And one of the ways in which we obtain the Christmas spirit—the Christ spirit—is by willingly giving of ourselves to others.

THE SON OF GOD

*For unto us a child is born, unto us a son is given: and
the government shall be upon his shoulder: and his name
shall be called Wonderful, Counsellor, The mighty
God, The everlasting Father, The Prince of Peace.*

ISAIAH 9:6

We remember with gratitude that night of
nights which marked the fulfillment of prophecy when a lowly manger cradled a newborn
child. With the birth of the babe in Bethlehem,
there emerged a great endowment, a power
stronger than weapons, a wealth more lasting
than the coins of Caesar. This child, born in
such primitive circumstances, was to be the
King of Kings and the Lord of Lords, the
promised Messiah—even Jesus Christ, the Son
of God.

OUR GREATEST FIELD OF ENJOYMENT

In all labour there is profit.

PROVERBS 14:23

What the public takes for brilliance is really the result of thorough, painstaking investigation and downright hard work. Were we to be deprived of work, we should be robbed of our greatest field of enjoyment and be forever condemned to mediocrity.

IS THERE ROOM
FOR HIM?

And she brought forth her firstborn son, and wrapped
him in swaddling clothes, and laid him in a manger;
because there was no room for them in the inn.

LUKE 2:7

As I drive through the many parts of this land, as I see the homes of America, I note that most homes have a room for Mary, a room for John—bedrooms, eating rooms, playrooms, sewing rooms—but I ask the fundamental question, "Is there room for the Son of Almighty God, our Savior, and our Redeemer?"

The invitation of the Lord is directed to each of us: "Behold, I stand at the door, and knock: if any man hear my voice, and open the door, I will come in to him" (Revelation 3:20).

OUT OF NAZARETH

And Nathanael said unto him,
Can there any good thing come out of Nazareth?
Philip saith unto him, Come and see.

JOHN 1:46

Can any good thing come out of Nazareth?

From Nazareth came example.

From Nazareth came sight.

From Nazareth came strength.

From Nazareth came life.

From Nazareth came faith.

From Nazareth came peace.

From Nazareth came courage.

From Nazareth came Christ.

To him Nathanael declared, "Thou art the Son of God; thou art the King of Israel" (John 1:49). I testify that he is a Lord of lords, King of kings, precious Savior, dear Redeemer. Jesus Christ of Nazareth. There is none other.

KEEPING CHRISTMAS

For the fruit of the Spirit is in
all goodness and righteousness and truth.

EPHESIANS 5:9

Our opportunities to give of ourselves are indeed limitless, but they are also perishable. There are hearts to gladden. There are kind words to say. There are gifts to be given. There are deeds to be done. There are souls to be saved. "Go, gladden the lonely, the dreary; Go, comfort the weeping, the weary; Go, scatter kind deeds on your way; Oh, make the world brighter today!" ("Make the World Brighter," *Deseret Sunday School Songs*, no. 197). A wise Christian once urged, "May we not spend Christmas, but keep it." When we keep the spirit of Christmas, we keep the spirit of Christ, for the Christmas spirit is the Christ spirit.

The Light of the World

For God so loved the world, that he gave his only begotten Son, that whosoever believeth in him should not perish, but have everlasting life.

John 3:16

With the pure love of Christ, let us walk in His footsteps as we approach the season celebrating His birth. As we do so, let us remember that He still lives and continues to be the "light of the world," who promised, "He that followeth me shall not walk in darkness, but shall have the light of life" (John 8:12).

With the spirit of Christ in our lives, we will have good will and love toward all mankind, not only during this season, but throughout the year as well.

A Thought for the Season

But whosoever drinketh of the water that
I shall give him shall never thirst; but the water
that I shall give him shall be in him a well of
water springing up into everlasting life.

JOHN 4:14

At this joyous season, may personal discords be forgotten and animosities healed. May enjoyment of the season include remembrance of the needy and afflicted. May our forgiveness reach out to those who have wronged us, even as we hope to be forgiven. May goodness abound in our hearts and love prevail in our homes.

As we contemplate how we're going to spend our money to buy gifts this holiday season, let us plan also for how we will spend our time in order to help bring the true spirit of Christmas into the lives of others.

A MODEL TO FOLLOW

Never did any passage of scripture come
with more power to the heart of man than this
did at this time to mine. It seemed to enter with
great force into every feeling of my heart.

JOSEPH SMITH—HISTORY 1:12

No description of models for us to follow would be complete without including Joseph Smith, the first prophet of this dispensation. When but fourteen years of age, this courageous young man entered a grove of trees, which later would be called sacred, and received an answer to his sincere prayer. There followed for Joseph unrelenting persecution as he related to others the account of the glorious vision he received in that grove. Yet, although he was ridiculed and scorned, he stood firm. Said he, "I had seen a vision; I knew it, and I knew that God knew it, and I could not deny it, neither dared I do it" (Joseph Smith—History 1:25).

TURNING OUR HEARTS TO CHRIST

*Where is he that is born King of
the Jews? for we have seen his star in the
east, and are come to worship him.*

MATTHEW 2:2

This is a glorious time of the year, simple in origin, deep in meaning, beautiful in tradition and custom, rich in memories, and charitable in spirit. It has an attraction to which our hearts are readily drawn. This joyful season brings to each of us a measure of happiness that corresponds to the degree in which we have turned our minds, feelings, and actions to the Spirit of Christmas.

SEEK THE STAR

When they had heard the king,
they departed; and, lo, the star, which they saw
in the east, went before them, till it came and
stood over where the young child was.

MATTHEW 2:9

May we give as the Savior gave. To give of oneself is a holy gift. We give as a remembrance of all the Savior has given. May we also give gifts that have eternal value, along with our gifts that eventually break or are forgotten. How much better the world would be if we all gave gifts of understanding and compassion, of service and friendship, of kindness and gentleness. As the Christmas season envelops us with all its glory, may we, as did the Wise Men, seek a bright, particular star to guide us in our celebration of the Savior's birth. May we all make the journey to Bethlehem in spirit, taking with us a tender, caring heart as our gift to the Savior.

STILL A
BRIGHT STAR

His lord said unto him, Well done,
thou good and faithful servant: thou hast been
faithful over a few things, I will make thee ruler over
many things: enter thou into the joy of thy lord.

MATTHEW 25:21

We remember that during the meridian of time a bright, particular star shone in the heavens. Wise men followed it and found the Christ child. Today wise men still look heavenward and again see a bright, particular star. It will guide you and me to our opportunities. The burden of the downtrodden will be lifted, the cry of the hungry stilled, the lonely heart comforted. And souls will be saved—yours, theirs, and mine.

If we truly listen, we may hear that voice from far away say to us, as it spoke to another, "Well done, thou good and faithful servant."

BE OF
GOOD CHEER

*I came forth from the Father, and
am come into the world: again, I leave
the world, and go to the Father.*

JOHN 16:28

The Lord admonished, "Be of good cheer; I have overcome the world" (John 16:33). What great happiness this knowledge should bring to us. He lived for us and He died for us. He paid the price for our sins. May we emulate His example. May we show our great gratitude to Him by accepting His sacrifice and living lives that will qualify us to return and one day live with Him.

YOUR PATRIARCHAL BLESSING

And he took them up in his arms,
put his hands upon them, and blessed them.

MARK 10:16

Help in maintaining the proper perspective in these permissive times can come to you from many sources. One valuable resource is your patriarchal blessing. Read it frequently. Study it carefully. Be guided by its cautions. Live to merit its promises. If you have not yet received your patriarchal blessing, plan for the time when you will receive it, and then cherish it.

WHAT COULD HAVE BEEN

I will say of the Lord,
He is my refuge and my fortress:
my God; in him will I trust.

PSALM 91:2

Struggles across the globe remind us that the peace we seek will not come without effort and determination. Anger, hatred, and contention are foes not easily subdued. These enemies inevitably leave in their destructive wake tears of sorrow, the pain of conflict, and the shattered hopes of what could have been. Their sphere of influence is not restricted to the battlefields of war but can be observed altogether too frequently in the home, around the hearth, and within the heart. So soon do many forget and so late do they remember the counsel of the Lord.

"BE THOU AN EXAMPLE"

*For I have given you an example,
that ye should do as I have done to you.*

JOHN 13:15

Paul, in his epistle to his beloved Timothy, outlined a way whereby we could become our better selves and, at the same time, provide assistance to others who ponder or ask the question, "How can I [find my way], except some man should guide me?" (Acts 8:31).

The answer, given by Paul to Timothy, provides an inspired charge to each of us. Let us take heed of his wise counsel: "Be thou an example of the believers, in word, in conversation, in charity, in spirit, in faith, in purity" (1 Timothy 4:12).

WILL YOU HEAR?

*Having eyes, see ye not? and having ears,
hear ye not? and do ye not remember?*

MARK 8:18

There is no deafness so permanent as the deafness which will not hear. There is no blindness so incurable as the blindness which will not see. There is no ignorance so deep as the ignorance that will not know.

IMAGE CREDITS

January © Paul Aniszewski/Shutterstock.com

February © Mr_Twister/iStock/Thinkstock

March © Wrang/iStock/Thinkstock

April © Timmary/Shutterstock.com

May © ikontee/Shutterstock.com

June © B. and E. Dudzinscy/Shutterstock.com

July © Erik Wollo/Shutterstock.com

August © straga/Shutterstock.com
  and © ecco/Shutterstock.com

September © Igor Strukov/Shutterstock.com

October © Natata/Shutterstock.com
  and © valzan/Shutterstock.com

November © Sunny Forest/Shutterstock.com
  and © Dionisvera/Shutterstock.com

December © Henry Steven/Shutterstock.com
  and © seeyou/Shutterstock.com